The Inner Theatre of
Recent FRENCH POETRY

The Inner Theatre of
Recent FRENCH POETRY

CENDRARS
TZARA
PÉRET
ARTAUD
BONNEFOY *by Mary Ann Caws*

PRINCETON UNIVERSITY PRESS, NEW JERSEY

73- 79

LC Card: 72-166-364
ISBN: 0-691-06212-9

Publication of this book has been aided by
the Whitney Darrow Publication
Reserve Fund of Princeton University Press

Printed in the United States of America by
Princeton University Press

La mobilité délivre le chant,
le chant se fait immobilité sans
frein (courant dans un courant).
  PHILIPPE SOLLERS,
  Logiques

Mais le mouvement est-il plus
explicatif que l'immobilité?
  MANUEL DE DIÉGUEZ,
  Science et nescience

ACKNOWLEDGMENTS

I SHOULD like to thank the following journals for permission to reprint, in altered form, essays which have appeared in their pages: the *French Review* ("Artaud and the Myth of Motion," February 1968; "The 'Amour sublime' of Benjamin Péret: Just Another 'Amour fou'?" November 1966; and "Motion, Vision, and Coherence in the Early Dada Poetry of Tristan Tzara," Special issue no. 1, Winter 1970); *Kentucky Romance Quarterly* ("Blaise Cendrars: a Cinema of Poetry," Volume XVII, 4, 1970); *Romance Notes* ("Péret and the Surrealist Word," Volume 11, Number 2, 1969); *Symposium* ("Motion and Motion Arrested: the Language of the Surrealist Movement," Spring 1966); *Cahiers Dada Surréalisme* ("Dada's Interior Language as Exterior Manifestation," Number 4, 1972).

My thanks to the following publishers for their permission to quote copyright materials: Mercure de France for "L'Ordalie I, II" from Yves Bonnefoy, *Du Mouvement et de l'immobilité de Douve*, © 1953; Editions Seghers for "Atout trèfle," from *Benjamin Péret* (Poètes d'aujourd'hui), © 1961; and Editions Denoël

Acknowledgments

for "La Tour," from Blaise Cendrars, *Oeuvres complètes*, © 1947.

Without the resources of the Bibliothèque littéraire Jacques Doucet, the help of François Chapon, and the kind permission of Christophe Tzara to consult and refer to his father's manuscripts, I should not have been able to complete the chapter on Tristan Tzara.

Grants both from the George N. Shuster Faculty Fellowship Fund and from the Abbie and Nora Fund of Hunter College, as well as from the Research Foundation of the City University of New York (Fellowship number 1033), assisted in the research for and preparation of this manuscript.

My very warmest thanks go to my colleague Professor Hanna Charney, for her enlightened comments and her encouragement on this as on so many other occasions. I am deeply grateful to Yves Bonnefoy, and to Professor and Mrs. LeRoy Breunig for their generosity and interest. For his frequently solicited and much appreciated advice and for his enthusiastic support, my husband deserves a better acknowledgment than I am able to write.

New York, March 12 and May 12, 1971

CONTENTS

The Inner Theatre of
Recent FRENCH POETRY

INTRODUCTION

The Place and Play of the Poetic Text

CENTERING on the theme of motion and immobility in recent poetics, these essays deal with a number of movements, attitudes, and theories, including simultanism, Dada, surrealism, the Theatre of Cruelty, and a contemporary poetics of metaphysical intent. They touch on various aesthetic problems related to art, film, theory of game, and theatrical presentation, particularly in their connections with poetry. Moving from the vividly cinematic to a simplicity of line more contemplative than active, they illustrate greatly differing perspectives on motion and its cessation, on dynamic impulse and static fixation.

The first three essays stress the positive energy of movement, whereas the last three examine an underlying fascination with immobility and paralysis. Blaise Cendrars, representing the passion for adventure recounted (if not actually undertaken) and the practice as well as the theory of simultaneous contrast or simul-

3

taneous representation, which is closely allied to cinematic montage,[1] discusses the most direct of elements:
color, line and form, scope, depth, and size, all preoccupations of the most *exterior* meditation on movement. Representing Dada theory and a poetry of spectacle and spectacular rapidity, of the bright revolution
of the circus, Tristan Tzara's brief and vivid notes on
art and poetry insist on vitality, rhythm, and direction
as the component qualities of the linguistic gesture. Its
potential depends on the intimate association of those
qualities, its intensity on theirs. Benjamin Péret represents surrealist theory in its purest state of unending
adventure, together with what we have called an epic
poetry of illogic or of the marvelous, these terms being closely linked within the surrealist imagination.[2] Nor

[1] The *montage* necessitates a parallel systematic *découpage*
or truncation of the telescoped objects, so that the moment or
the vision signifies alone, with no outside reference. The relation
of this procedure to Cubist theory is clear, although Cendrars
repeatedly attacked the Cubist painters for what he saw as a
lack of depth.

[2] About the terms "theatre" and "epic" as they will be used
in these pages, two brief remarks should be made. As Pierre
Francastel observes in his *Peinture et société: Naissance et destruction d'un espace plastique de la renaissance au cubisme*
(Audin, 1951), the Renaissance individual thought himself an
efficacious agent, working with a fixed Euclidean perspective, so
that the mental and architectural space of the stage was felt to
be a stable one; whereas the modern space of art and of the
mind is not that at all, but rather a net of intersecting tensions,
of unstable currents. This is the conceptual basis for the motion
toward an inner theatre where the certain and the spectacular
gestures frequently give way to the implied and the hesitant
ones. And on this also depends the idea of the *epic gesture* to
which these pages allude: this gesture is the direct opposite of
Goethe's *outward* epic. It rather combines the tragic or inward-
tending, the mental journeying through space and time of an

4

should we separate Péret's poetic theory from his poems: both carry the same explosive charge. It is more certainly here than in any other case a matter of "one within the other," of all surrealist games the most characteristic and most far-reaching in its implications. In sum, this initial set of essays considers the spectacular rather than the meditative, is directed toward a range of exterior images as wide as it is colorful. The cinema of simultanism and the circus of Dada lead to the great game (Péret's *Grand jeu*), serious and brilliant, played and replayed by the surrealists, and "always for the first time." The poetic gesture is rapid, sure, and imparts no sense of menace.

For the starting point of the second half of the book, more theoretical and less spectacular in its orientation than the first, the relation between language and

---

uncertain and often "illogical" hero, the Eisensteinian collision of events not only shock-producing but destructive of stability and balance, and the Joycean notion of epic self-effacement. (For the latter, see Joseph Frank, *The Widening Gyre* [Rutgers, 1963], where there is also a clear discussion of one aspect of the space and time problem as it relates to contemporary literature and poetry.)

For the application to film, see Rudolf Arnheim, "Epic and Dramatic Film" in Richard MacKann, *Film: A Montage of Theories* (Dutton, 1966) and Sergei Eisenstein, *Film Sense* and *Film Form* (Harcourt, Brace, 1942 and 1949). For the idea of the kinetic poem, or poetry as motion, see Pierre Garnier, *Spatialisme et poésie concrète* (Gallimard, 1968), p. 123: "Donc un poème est dit cinétique s'il est en mouvement, c'est-à-dire s'il se forme, se transforme, se déforme, se forme, etc. sous nos yeux—qu'il se déplace virtuellement ou réellement." The active creation of the poem is said to fill all the space of the poem, which becomes an outpouring of energy: "Ni achèvement, ni inachèvement, un mouvement continu s'empare de l'auteur, du texte, du lecteur— et nous nous emparons du mouvement." (p. 144)

scene, text and gesture, is briefly discussed. Then the game is observed from another angle, as the *place* of the game is gradually moved inwards. As in the first part, the essays are arranged from the outside in, from the easiest to the most complicated and most theoretical. The central essay, forming the point of juncture between the first and second parts, examines the language of the surrealist adventure, which has undeniably set the tone for all the subsequent poetic adventure of our century. With the exception of Cendrars, all the poets discussed were surrealists at one time; from Tzara, whose Dada movement gave the first impetus to the discoveries of surrealism and who was himself associated with the surrealists for a number of years, to Bonnefoy, who claims and demonstrates an "interior faithfulness to surrealism,"[3] each of them shows in some manner traces of the attitudes and the styles of the surrealist experience.

The surrealist language, based on a will to movement and metamorphosis, depends on the clash of the mobile with the immobile just as surely as it does on the intimate and violent juxtaposition of the self (or the same) with the other. Thus a train, agent of the imagination, hurtles along on rails sticky with blue honey or, at other moments, rushes and continues to rush into a forest where it is, however, stopped at full speed. The extreme convulsiveness of the motion comes from its sudden forced halt; the illogical intensity, from the

[3] See his invaluable discussion of his own relation to surrealism and of its parallel tendencies toward totality and nothingness in the Surrealism issue of *Yale French Studies*, Spring, 1966.

impossible continuity. All the means of exterior voyage are eventually halted in the same fashion, and forever. Whether they *also* continue is only for the poet to say. Furthermore, the problem of openness and movement relates not only to the surrealist idea but—and more gravely—to the textual actuality. The poem of mobility fixed upon the page, the temporal space of adventure pinned to the wall in the image of a calendar, the heroes of adventure shipwrecked—why this insistence in surrealist works on closure, paralysis, catastrophe? The tentative answer given here, of necessity only partial, forms the pivotal point of the study. There is perhaps a limit to the reader's vision which does not coincide with the limit of the action within the text. At a certain moment, the gesture made for us as mere spectators may move inside, to another scene where only the actor is the judge. What appears to us as the tragic cessation of movement may serve, transferred, as the threshold for a new motion and a new theatre. The scene may be glimpsed now inside the text, beyond the traditional place of *play*.

The particular tragedy of Antonin Artaud, his private obsession with a mental motionlessness or the *impouvoir* of the paralyzed mind, demonstrates the unbridgable distance between the jerky but continuous movement of the Dada circus and the profound inhibitions haunting the space of the modern theatre. The burning realization of the self that the dramatic gesture was to have been turns now to a morbid consuming of that self and of that gesture; now the heroic yields to the pathetic, the theatre as spectacle to the theatre as cessation of motion. But a possible salvation is glimpsed in the concentration on the simplest and barest of images, on an aesthetic minimum, on a whole theatre of meaning visible in one line alone. In an extraordinary turning point, the violence of this tragic theatre is resumed, clarified, and illuminated in Artaud's profound meditation on the painter Uccello.

Finally, Yves Bonnefoy represents the most "metaphysical" of contemporary meditations on art, on painting in particular, where the force of the gesture is necessarily inscribed within a limited framework.[4] The complex interplay of that static outline with the momentum of the gesture has a parallel in the interwoven notions of presence and absence, speech and silence, perfection and imperfection, movement and the temp-

---

[4] For a more "structural" analysis of painting in its relation to game, gesture, object, language, and the position of the spectator or reader, see Michel Foucault, *Les Mots et les choses* (Gallimard, 1966) and Jean-Louis Schefer, *Scénographie d'un tableau* (Seuil, 1969). Of particular interest in the former is the opening analysis of a Velasquez painting, where a certain complexity of situation—the relations of spectator, artist, mirror, and canvas—is contrasted with a single opened window, and where the various kinds of vacancy (of absence, action, vision) lead to a final *pure* representation. The latter offers a complicated analysis of a chess game as the model for the painting in which it is pictured (Paris Bordone's "A Chess Game"): of a card game as the "degraded" intermediary between a strong stage of game, chess (with its parallel image of checkered tiles), and the neutral stage of nature; and of the canvas as a visual text, a *mise-en-scène* (or *mise-en-cadre*) to be read. The fact that this painting is classified as a double portrait gives it a further link with the notion of representation and doubling as it is discussed here. For the ideas of language and game, Schefer refers us to Saussure, Roussel, and Hjelmslev (note 11, p. 198).

tation to immobility which form the fabric of his poems, all of an apparent simplicity. Bonnefoy's quiet meditations have a transparency lent them by the space surrounding each gesture, each line. Or an illusion of transparency: the repeated motifs of ship, salamander, summer, stone, wind, and phoenix halt the linguistic movement by their recurring presence, while they confer on the texts a deep seriousness, a profundity attainable only by repetition and slow metamorphosis. For here the motion has come almost to a standstill, and we are at the opposite pole from Cendrars, Tzara, and Péret.

A major poet and a major critic, Bonnefoy, more than any other of the writers discussed here, has the exceptional talent of raising a single word to the level of a poetic statement, of making a single object perceived— a withered leaf, a salamander—into an entire canvas of homage to time passing and to the present moment. His studies of the poetic gesture, whether painted or spoken, are no less solemn than his poetry itself; they translate to a different plane of meaning and of vision the contemplation of the work. Now the exterior brilliance captured by the moving camera, enclosed in the circus ring or in the marvelous rules of the epic game, has passed through the stage of paradox and self-examination, through the public anguish of theatre and the private anguish of poetry, through the diffusion of signs and colored forms on the canvas to reach at last an inner and metaphysical space, accessible only through the text (in itself a whole theatre or one line), but not confined to it. This gesture, as subtle as it is profound, takes its point of departure from a theatre of motion but finds its true place beyond the eternal immobility of painting.

And yet, within the language of arrested movement, we sense a continuing motion, as within the violent spectacle of the poets of action there runs a certain current of fear and fatigue, betrayed by the occasional halting gesture. These essays are intended as studies of the moving and unmoving gesture or language within a few texts on which we may confer, in the particular sense discussed here, the name of theatre.

No apologies will be made for the implied theoretical basis necessarily underlying the free use of terms such as "poetic gesture," "linguistic gesture," "theatre of language," and the like. The traditional barriers or boundaries holding between the notions of verbal and physical actions or among the genres of poetry, theatre, and drama are presumed to hold no longer. That is part, and an essential part, of the specific modernity of the gesture, or its "modernism."[5]

[5] See such works as Irving Howe, ed., *Literary Modernism* (Fawcett, 1967), R. P. Blackmur, *Language as Gesture* (Harcourt, Brace, 1952), Kenneth Burke, *The Philosophy of Literary Form: Studies in Symbolic Action* (Vintage, 1957), etc. From Blackmur: "Gesture, in language, is the outward and dramatic play of inward and imaged meaning. It is that play of meaningfulness among words which cannot be defined in the formulas in the dictionary, but which is defined in their use together; gesture is that meaningfulness which is moving, in every sense of that word: what moves the words and what moves us." (p. 6) "It is the gesture, I like to think, of poetic judgement, the judgement of all the gestures, all the play of meaning, which makes up full being. Poetry is the meaning of meaning, or at least the

Finally, the position taken in the following chapters is that the expansion of meaning and the opening of form brought about by the internalizing and the intensifying of linguistic gesture in its theatrically ambiguous mobile immobility should be called *poetic*, a term appropriate to scene, to language, to action, and to attitude. These are, then, essays on motion and on a space at once the ground for a poetic theatre and for a genuine theatre of poetry.

---

prophecy of it." (p. 12) "In a sense any word or congeries of words can be pushed to the condition of gesture either by simple repetition or by a combination of repetition and varied preparation." (p. 13)

PREFATORY TEXTS

As is often the case with commentaries on contemporary poetry, the text and concern for the text precede any method of analysis. It seems only fair, therefore, to offer a brief example from the texts of each writer selected here in order to indicate the *textual* atmosphere within which the following essays were written. These extracts were chosen as both typical of the writers' work and characteristic of our particular concern with motion and its cessation.

They are arranged, like the chapters, from the more optimistic, active, and exterior—towers and turning, arrows climbing to astral heights, adventures over mountains and obstacles overcome—to a more mental adventure, the paralysis of the mind, and the deliberate halt and limitation—from the phantom ships of the mind to the ship trapped in the ice floes, ships and persons stranded on beaches of dry bones, and ships sailing at last into port. The road leading from Cendrars to Bonnefoy is the possible scene for an adventure of the first poetic magnitude.

LA TOUR

1910
Castellamare
Je dînais d'une orange à l'ombre d'un oranger
Quand, tout à coup. . .
    O Tour Eiffel
Feu d'artifice géant de l'Exposition Universelle!
Sur le Gange
À Bénarès
Parmi les toupies onanistes des temples hindous
Et les cris colorés des multitudes de l'Orient
Tu te penches, gracieux Palmier!
. . .
Au coeur de l'Afrique c'est toi qui cours
Girafe
Autruche
Boa
Equateur
Moussons
En Australie tu as toujours été tabou
Tu es la gaffe que le capitaine Cook employait
   pour diriger son bateau d'aventuriers
Ô sonde céleste!
Pour le Simultané Delaunay, à qui je dédie ce poème,
Tu es le pinceau qu'il trempe dans la lumière

Gong tam-tam Zanzibar bête de la jungle rayons-X
   express bistouri symphonie
Tu es tout
Tour
Dieu antique

Bête moderne
Spectre solaire
Sujet de mon poème
Tout
Tour du monde
Tour en mouvement

> Blaise Cendrars (1913) from
> *Dix-neuf poèmes élastiques*

TOWER

1910
Castellamare
I was dining on an orange in the shadow of an
  orange-tree
When, suddenly. . .
  Oh Eiffel Tower
Gigantic fireworks of the World's Fair!
On the Ganges
At Benares
Among the onanist tops of Hindu temples
And the bright-hued cries of Oriental multitudes
You bend, oh graceful Palm!
. . .
In the heart of Africa you run
Giraffe
Ostrich
Boa
Equator
Monsoons
Always forbidden in Australia

14

Captain Cook used you for a hook to guide his ship of
adventurers
Oh celestial probe!
For the Simultanist Delaunay to whom I dedicate
this poem
You are the paintbrush he dips in light

Gong tom-tom Zanzibar jungle beast x-rays express
scalpel symphony
You are everything
Tower
God of old
Modern beast
Solar spectre
Subject of my poem
Everything
Tower of the world tour
Tower in motion turning

NOTE SUR LA POÉSIE

Le poète de la station dernière ne pleure plus inutile-
ment, la plainte ralentit la marche. Humidité des âges
passés. Ceux qui se nourrissent de larmes sont con-
tents et lourds, ils les enfilent pour tromper les ser-
pents derrière les colliers de leurs âmes. Le poète peut
s'adonner à des exercices de gymnastique suédoise.
Mais pour l'abondance et l'explosion, il sait allumer
l'espoir AUJOURD'HUI. Tranquille, ardent, furieux,
intime, pathétique, lent, impétueux, son désir bout
pour l'enthousiasme, féconde forme de l'intensité.

Savoir reconnaître et cueillir les traces de la force que nous attendons, qui sont partout, dans une langue essentielle de chiffres, gravées sur les cristaux, sur les coquillages, les rails, dans les nuages, dans le verre, à l'intérieur de la neige, de la lumière, sur le charbon, la main, dans les rayons qui se groupent autour des pôles magnétiques, sur les ailes.

La persistance aiguise et fait monter la joie en flèche vers les cloches astrales, distillation des vagues de nourriture impassible, créatrice d'une vie nouvelle.

. . .

Sous l'écorce des arbres abattus, je cherche la peinture des choses à venir, de la vigueur et dans les canaux la vie gonfle peut-être, déjà, l'obscurité du fer et du charbon.

Tristan Tzara (in Dada 4 and 5, 1919)

Note on poetry

The poet of the last station no longer weeps in vain, lamentation would slow him down. Humidity of ages past. Those who feed on tears are heavy and content, they string them like beads to deceive the snakes lurking behind the necklaces of their souls. The poet can practice Swedish gymnastics if he likes. But for abundance and explosion he knows how to light hope TODAY. Tranquil, ardent, furious, intimate, pathetic, slow, impetuous, his desire boils for enthusiasm, fecund form of intensity.

To know how to recognize and gather the traces of the strength we are waiting for, traces which are found everywhere, in an essential language of numbers, engraved in crystals, in seashells, train tracks, clouds, glass, inside snow, inside light, in coal, in the hand, in the rays grouped around magnetic poles, on wings.

Persistence sharpens joy and sends it up in arrows toward the astral bells, distillation of waves of impassive nourishment, creator of a new life.

. . .

Under the bark of felled trees I seek the painting of things to come, vigor, and in the canals life is taking shape perhaps already, the darkness of iron and coal.

ATOUT TRÈFLE

Assemble la pierre de l'élan brisé et l'erreur des
    branches au fil de l'eau
Doute de l'horizon de l'autre côté de tes yeux
et va-t-en à travers les montagnes blanches de
    fougères
. . .
le misérable coquillage de la route se déroulera
    comme une ceinture de sauvetage
une ceinture qui ne sauve que les suicidés aux
    mains de flamme
debout sur les collines qui rient
car tes collines des suicidés rient d'un rire de chute
    d'eau
avec des vis dans leur voix de fumée
et des escaliers infinis dans leurs gestes
qui s'égarent dans les boules bleues du temps perdu
Celui qui n'a pas perdu son temps dans les soupapes
    de la neige

17

ne connaît pas la force dissolvante de l'aubépine
fleurie baignant dans le sable blond
ni le courage désespéré des petites rivières
traversant des marais d'armoiries
Et celui qui n'a pas senti le regard prismatique des
palmiers
se poser sur l'épine dorsale de l'avoine
dont la chute correspond au degré de torréfaction
du café
celui-là ne sait pas ce que c'est que le vent perdu
et ne peut prétendre qu'à l'oubli
au plus définitif oubli des cils battants
à moins que son souffle sursaute
au passage affolé des murailles mordues par les
écorces tombantes
qu'anime la colère des obstacles surmontés

Benjamin Péret (from *De Derrière
les fagots*, 1934)

SPADES ARE TRUMPS

Assemble the stone of the shattered gesture and the
error of branches sweeping with the stream
Suspect the horizon on the other side of your eyes
and depart across the mountains white with fern
. . .
the miserable seashell of the road will unroll like a
safety belt
a belt to save only the suicides with flaming hands
standing on the hills laughing
for your hills of suicides laugh with a waterfall of
laughter

with screws in their voice of smoke
and infinite stairs in their gestures
which are lost in the blue balls of lost time
He who has not lost time in the valves of snow
cannot know the solvent force of the flowering
   hawthorn bathing in blond sand
or the desperate courage of little rivers crossing
   armory swamps
And he who has not felt the palm trees' prismatic
   gaze
come to rest on the spine of the hay
whose slope answers in degree to the temperature
   of roasting coffee
he cannot know the lost wind
claiming only definite forgetfulness
forgetfulness of batting lashes
unless his breath catches
at the crazed passing of the walls bitten by falling
   bark
animated by the anger of obstacles overcome

LE POINT DE LA MORT

Navigateur du silence, le dock est sans couleur et
sans forme ce quai d'où partira ce soir le beau vaisseau fantôme, ton esprit.

. . .

Le vaisseau fantôme écrit sa danse en plein ciel. Les
murs s'écartent entre lesquels on voulut enchaîner
les vents de l'esprit. Derrière les plis d'un velours trop
lourdement paisible s'allume un soleil de soufre et
d'amour. Les hommes du monde entier se compren-

nent par le nez. Un geyser imprévu envoie au diable des pierres dont on a tenté d'habiller le sol. Il y a un pont de la planète minuscule à la liberté.

Du point de la mort, venez voir, venez tous voir la fête qui s'allume.

René Crevel (in *La Révolution surréaliste*, no. 7, 1926)

THE POINT OF DEATH

Navigator of silence, the dock is colorless and formless the wharf whence the beautiful phantom ship of your mind departs tonight.

. . .

The phantom ship writes its dance on the sky. The walls between which the winds of the mind were to be chained withdraw. Behind the folds of a velvet too heavily placid a sun is lit of sulphur and love. All over the world men communicate by intuition. An unexpected geyser sends off into the distance the rocks the soil was to be dressed in. A bridge stretches from the minuscule planet over to liberty.

From the point of death, come to see, all of you come to see the celebration lighting up.

LA BAIE DE LA FAIM

Navire en bois d'ébène parti pour le pôle Nord voici que la mort se présente sous la forme d'une baie circulaire et glaciale, sans pingouins, sans phoques, sans ours. Je sais quelle est l'agonie d'un navire pris dans la banquise, je connais le râle froid et la mort pharaonique des explorateurs arctiques et antarctiques, avec ses anges rouges et verts et le scorbut et la peau brûlée par le froid. D'une capitale d'Europe, un journal emporté par un vent du sud monte rapidement vers le pôle en grandissant et ses deux feuilles sont deux grandes ailes funèbres.

Robert Desnos (from *La Liberté ou l'amour!* 1927)

THE BAY OF HUNGER

Ebony ship set off for the North Pole, now death appears in the form of a circular glacial bay without penguins, without seals, without bears. I know the anguish of a ship caught in the ice floes, I know the cold death rattle and the Pharaoh's fate granted to arctic and antarctic explorers, with red and green angels and scurvy and frostbitten skin. From a capital of Europe, a newspaper lifted by a south wind climbs rapidly toward the pole increasing in size and its two sheets are two great funereal wings.

L'ENCLUME DES FORCES

. . .

Chiens, avez vous fini de rouler vos galets sur mon âme. Moi. Moi. Tournez la page des gravats. Moi aussi j'espère le gravier céleste et la plage qui n'a plus de bords. Il faut que ce feu commence à moi. Ce feu et ces langues, et les cavernes de ma gestation. Que les blocs de glace reviennent s'échouer sous mes dents. J'ai le crâne épais, mais l'âme lisse, un coeur de matière échouée. J'ai absence de météores, absence de soufflets enflammés. Je cherche dans mon gosier des noms, et comme le cil vibratile des choses. L'odeur du néant, un relent d'absurde, le fumier de la mort entière. . . . L'humour léger et raréfié. Moi aussi je n'attends que le vent. Qu'il s'appelle amour ou misère, il ne pourra guère m'échouer que sur une plage d'ossements.

> Antonin Artaud (*La Révolution surréaliste*, no. 8, 1926, reprinted in *L'Art et la Mort*, 1929)

ANVIL OF FORCES

. . .

Dogs, have you finished rolling your boulders across my soul. Myself. Myself. Turn the page of rubbish. I too await the celestial gravel and the limitless beaches. This fire must start with me. This fire and these tongues, and the caverns of my gestation. Let blocks of ice strand themselves under my teeth at their return. I have a thick skull but a smooth soul, a heart of stranded matter. I have an absence of meteors, an absence of bellows aflame. I seek names in my throat, and as it were the vibrating eyelash of things. The odor of nothingness, a stench of the absurd, the dungheap of death in its completeness. . . . Humor light and rarefied. I too am waiting only for wind. Let its name be love or misery, it shall never strand me except on a beach of dry bones.

L'Ordalie

I

J'étais celui qui marche par souci
D'une eau dernière trouble. Il faisait beau

Dans l'été le plus clair. Il faisait nuit
De toujours et sans borne et pour toujours.

Dans la glaise des mers
Le chrysanthème de l'écume et c'était toujours
La même odeur terreuse et fade de novembre
Quand je foulais le noir jardin des morts.

Il y avait
Qu'une voix demandait d'être crue, et toujours
Elle se retournait contre soi et toujours
Faisait de se tarir sa grandeur et sa preuve.

II

Je ne sais pas si je suis vainqueur. Mais j'ai saisi
D'un grand coeur l'arme enclose dans la pierre.
J'ai parlé dans la nuit de l'arme, j'ai risqué
Le sens et au-delà du sens le monde froid.

Un instant tout manqua,
Le fer rouge de l'être ne troua plus
La grisaille du verbe,
Mais enfin le feu se leva,
Le plus violent navire
Entra au port.

Aube d'un second jour,
Je suis enfin venu dans ta maison brûlante
Et j'ai rompu ce pain où l'eau lointaine coule.

> Yves Bonnefoy (from *Du Mouvement
> et de l'immobilité de Douve*, 1953)

Ordeal

I

It was I who walked with concern
For a last troubled water. It was fine weather
In the clearest summer. It was a night
Of always and without end and for always.

In the clay of seas
The chrysanthemum of foam and it was always
The same washed-out November smell of earth
When I trampled the black garden of the dead.

There was
A voice asking to be believed, and always
It turned against itself and always
Made of its hush its greatness and its trial.

II

I do not know if I am the victor. But I have seized
Willingly the sword enclosed in the stone.
I have spoken in the night of the sword, have risked
Meaning and beyond it the chill of the world.

For a moment everything lacked.
The red iron of being no longer punctured
The grayness of the word.
But at last the fire arose,
The most violent ship
Entered its port.

Dawn of a second day,
I have come at last into your burning house
And I have broken this bread wherein the far-off
    water runs.

SPECTACLE AND
OUTWARD MOVEMENT

Tzara, Cendrars, and Péret would seem at first glance the opposites of Artaud and Bonnefoy, the profound writers finally discussed. Their poetry appears to be determined more by a passion for spectacle than by a deep obsession, to be more superficial than significant. But from the circus of Dada and the cinema of simultaneity come important statements on the nature of language and on the cohesion of vision; moreover, the circular images of Tzara and the spiraling images of Cendrars are the perfect representations of poetic language in motion. As a conclusion to this section, the game of poetry, which Péret plays better than any other poet does, leads us to consider the juxtaposition of the geometrical *place*—sublime and necessary—with the gestures of liberal *provocation*, as the game combines the control of fixed rules with the freedom of spontaneous motion.

Here, in the game of Péret's poetry, the rapidity of the multiple verbal transpositions reveals a slippage (*glissement*) corresponding stylistically to all the images of surrealist adventure freely undertaken. This poetic statement of the marvelous played out is the perfect expression of the speed and the intensity of surrealist perception.

A. *Blaise Cendrars: A Cinema of Poetry*

Danse avec ta langue, Poète, fais un entrechat
Un tour de piste
  "Académie Médrano" *Sonnets dénaturés*

The starting point for these essays on motion is the work of a poet who sought the possibility of continuous gesture, who fled mental imprisonment (and to some extent, geographical limits—although in a less drastic manner than he would have had us think) at the eventual sacrifice of a certain poetic complexity.

1. ROAD

Blaise Cendrars concerned himself almost exclusively with the life of adventure and with the recounting of that adventure. The rough and varying surface of his writing is an appropriate medium for the transmission of his multiple experiences and their rapid succession. Describing himself as always in motion, Cendrars explains his obedience to

this need to flee which has so often taken hold of me, forcing me to make eccentric gestures and to take

26

extreme resolutions as sudden as they were unpre-meditated, to gamble heavily even to the point of death, waking up exhausted but absurdly ecstatic, whether at the limit of an impasse or in full flight, but never regretting anything or missing anyone and al-ways extraordinarily happy and proud of what I had just sacrificed, while at the same time poking fun at myself, and although uplifted by the intoxicating sen-sation of being lost or of setting off into a new world, having acquired a new body, despising myself each time a trifle more for having been taken in and for still believing in life.[1]

The long breathless sentence is appropriate to the ob-session with movement which informs all his writing and his life, a continued coming and going, a "vaga-

[1] Blaise Cendrars, *Vol à voile* (La Petite Ourse, 1931), pp. 88-89. The discovery that a good part of Cendrars' voyages were fables should not disconcert us: he made no attempt to hide his ideas of the relation between writing and doing. In a series of interviews ranging over a number of years and collected by Hughes Richard, *Dites-nous, Monsieur Blaise Cendrars* (Editions Rencontre, 1969), we find him defining his work in one word as "l'irréalisme," preferring above all other heroes Parsifal, Don Quixote, and Robinson Crusoe, and above all other faults that of lying. As for his attitude toward himself, "Je ne me prends pas au sérieux, je ne prends pas mes bouquins au sérieux. . . ." (p. 158) A sentence to be read in his *Inédits secrets* (présenta-tion de Miriam Cendrars, Club français du livre, 1969, p. 373) from a letter to Smirnoff of December 23, 1913, gives a succinct description of the value Cendrars attached to the voyage, real or imagined, and of its relation to art: "Le voyage est pour moi ce que vous appelez couleurs simultanées." To be noted, although in a lighter vein: Cendrars called his dog "Wagon-Lit" (see the picture in *Blaise Cendrars: 1887-1961*, Mercure de France, 1962).

bondage spécial."[2] Cendrars defines the "dance" of the poet as that of a metaphysical Don Juan who, having forsaken the misplaced pride and the spiritual poverty of literature, throws off his tedious habits for a restless life, literature's opposite.

The epic "Prose du Transsibérien et de la petite Jeanne de France" (1913) encompasses a journey of great physical complexity, geographical scope, and psychological melancholy. In the highly poetic "Prose,"[3] Cendrars repeatedly laments that in his "ardent and foolish" adolescence he was a bad poet, not knowing how to push himself to the limits of the possible. In the present, he can say of his life that it is, and has always been, in perpetual motion, that it has been measured out by train tracks. But even now he confesses his incapacity for the extremes of adventure: "Les lointains sont par trop loin." (I, 37) And the lament which might have been confined to his adolescence recurs insistently, like the stages of his journey:

Car je ne sais pas aller jusqu'au bout
Et j'ai peur (I, 41)

(For I don't know how to go all the way
And am afraid)

---

[2] Blaise Cendrars, *Du Monde entier, Poésies complètes: 1912-1924*; *Au Coeur du monde, Poésies complètes: 1924-29* (both, Gallimard, 1967). (Referred to in text as volumes I or II; reference here is to I, 81.)

[3] In his *Aujourd'hui* (Grasset, 1931), Cendrars uses parts of the "Prose" to exemplify the *lapsus linguae* used as a poetic technique. Here he refers to the work of the linguist Vendryes.

Cendrars explains, in the letter to Smirnoff already quoted from the *Inédits*, that he uses "prose" here in the sense of "prosa,

The railroad perfectly expresses the new geometry in its sharpness of contour and material hardness; the poet traveling along it has deliberately put himself in harmony with the life about him, and therefore takes a justifiable kind of pride in his modernity and in the cosmic value of his poetry thus cut off from the old static literature. Cendrars makes a broad claim in "Le Panama ou les aventures de mes sept oncles," another poem of epic scope, but often directed toward the nature of poetry itself:[4]

Ce matin est le premier jour du monde
. . .
La poésie date d'aujourd'hui
> La voie lactée autour du cou
> Les deux hémisphères sur les yeux
> À toute vitesse
> Il n'y a plus de pannes (I, 65)

(This morning is the world's first day
. . .
Poetry starts today
> The milky way around my neck
> Both hemispheres over my eyes
> Full speed ahead
> No more breakdowns)

Such unbounded optimism in the journey and the means of journey would seem unconquerable, but once

---

dictu." "Poème me semblait trop prétentieux, trop fermé. Prose est plus ouvert, populaire." (p. 371)

[4] Here the resemblance between these lines and the futurist attitude is striking. See footnote 8 to this chapter.

again, toward the end of this poem, Cendrars reveals his weakness and his fear:

Je suis tous les visages et j'ai peur des boîtes aux
   lettres
Les villes sont des ventres
Je ne suis plus les voies
Lignes
     Câbles
          Canaux
               Ni les ponts suspendus! (I, 66)[5]

(I follow all the faces and letterboxes frighten me
Towns are changed to stomachs
I no longer follow the paths
Lines
     Cables
          Canals
               Or suspension bridges!)

Predominant among the three essential psychological and aesthetic attitudes which can be distinguished here is the highly developed sensitivity, unmistakably expressed also in his "Prose du Transsibérien." In his poetry and his essays he repeatedly alludes to this characteristic, defining it as an element of the modern attitude, in both the personal and the impersonal realms, and thereby consecrating it as supremely valuable: "Je suis l'autre/Trop sensible," "Je suis empalé sur ma sensibilité," "Tout se sensibilise." His refusal to con-

---

[5] At the end of "Le Bateau ivre," Rimbaud, refusing to repeat in the future the sort of journey he has just completed, cries: "Je ne puis plus . . . nager sous les yeux horribles des pontons."

tinue his poetic tourism because the seen is in fact
pathetically undifferentiated, as the lines of railroads,
cables, and canals foster in their similarity a tedium of
the same, is now accompanied by a rejection of his former passivity. Before this, he had only *followed* the
lines of the countryside presented to him as a tourist in
his linear passage.

"Ma Danse," the poem of 1914 which opened this discussion and which forms the central image for all the
works of Cendrars as he places himself "au coeur du
monde," concludes with parallel statements on the
ennui of sameness and on the possible interest of a new
kind of motion, more circular than linear. The dance
of the landscape finally merges with his own, as the
pejorative sense of the notion *tourisme* (superficiality,
unoriginality of vision) yields to the more positive sense
of *tour* and *tourner*: the whirling motion of the seen
and of the seer suggests the idea of the universal with
which the poem ends:

> Je suis un monsieur qui en des express fabuleux
> traverse les toujours mêmes Europes et regarde
> decouragé par la portière
> Le paysage ne m'intéresse plus
> Mais la danse du paysage
> La danse du paysage
> Danse-paysage
> Paritatitata
> Je tout-tourne (I, 82)

> (I'm a gentleman who in fabulous express trains
> crosses Europes always the same

gazing out the window half-heartedly
The landscape interests me no longer
But the landscape's dance
The landscape's dance
Dance-landscape
Paritatitata
I am all-turning)

Flat spectacle is always uninteresting and similar to itself; the interest lies in the clacking of the train wheels down the linear track as it contrasts with the spinning of the landscape and the poet together. On this spinning gesture Cendrars will base the greater part of his poetry.

2. LINE AND SPIRAL

"THE SPIRAL, symbol of freedom of falling of life in the center of the universe as it opens out."[6] More often

[6] Blaise Cendrars, *Le Lotissement du ciel* (Denöel, 1949), p. 244. (*L*) As Francis Carmody points out in his *Cubist Poetry* (Berkeley, 1954, no publisher listed), Paul Dermée's poems called *Spirales* of 1917 are paratactic in their structure, like Cendrars' own.
Compare the following lines of one of these poems (exhibited at "The Cubist Epoch," Metropolitan Museum of New York, Spring 1971), which are as close in tone and spectacle to Tzara's poetry of the same years as they are to Cendrars'. The jump-rope of the little girl ("ô toi qui sautes") lends its parabolic form and its jerky tempo to the rhythmic arrangement:

Souffle ton haleine sur l'oiseau tombée du toit
C'est ta mission

fille à la corde
Ce souffle froid qui vient du corridor. . . .
Serpent qui passe sous tes bottines
villes   campagnes
fleuves gonflés de pluie

than any other geometrical figure, that of the spiral recurs in Cendrars' prose and poetry. He associates it with profundity and with an intense presence. Although the unilinear voyage disappoints him by its monotony and its superficial nature, there is another possibility to which he attaches all the values of the total as well as the deep. "On vit dans la profondeur. On voyage dans la profondeur. J'y suis. Les sens y sont. Et l'esprit."[7] (We live in depth. We travel in depth. I am there. The senses also. And the mind.) In his essay on the simultanist painter Delaunay, one of the brilliant series of commentaries on painters, poets, and the modern spirit called *Aujourd'hui* ("Profond aujourd'hui," "Tout autour d'aujourd'hui") Cendrars states his objections to the cubists, based on their consideration of the lines of objects rather than of reality itself, in its depth. The spiral of the whirlwind is a primary image both in his lyric appreciation of the modern spirit ("Prodigieux

---

Saute et danse
la terre tourne sous tes pieds
Tu plânes au milieu des étoiles
JEUNESSE MÉTÉORE DES NUITS D'ÉTÉ

(Blow your breath on the bird fallen from the roof
It's your mission
girl with a jump-rope
This cold breath coming from the corridor. . . .
Snake slithering under your boots
towns   countrysides
rivers swollen with rain
Leap and dance
the earth spins under your feet
You hover in the center of stars
YOUTH METEOR OF SUMMER NIGHTS)

[7] Blaise Cendrars, *Aujourd'hui*, p. 128. (A)

33

aujourd'hui. Sonde. Antenne. Porte-visage-tourbillon. Tu vis. Excentrique. . . . Le moteur tourne en spirale. Le rythme parle. Chimisme. Tu es."/Prodigious today. Probe. Antenna. Door-face-tornado. You live. Eccentric. . . . The motor turns in a spiral. Rhythm speaks. Chemistry. You are.—from "Profond aujourd'hui" *A,* 17) and in his homage to the cinema, from the same collection of essays ("Le Cinéma. Tourbillon des mouvements dans l'espace. Tout tombe. Le soleil tombe. Nous tombons à sa suite. . . . Fusion. Tout s'ouvre, s'écroule, se fonde aujourd'hui, se creuse, se dresse, s'épanouit."/ The Cinema. Tornado of motion in space. Everything falls. The sun falls. We fall after it. . . . Fusion. Everything opens, crumbles, melts today, digs, pulls itself up, opens out.—from "L'ABC du cinéma" *A,* 55). The whirling spiral is seen here as closely related to the value of verticality ("tout tombe") and of the profound operations of chemistry as opposed to the surface mechanical workings which Cendrars finds characteristic of the futurists. By extension, the rhythm of which it is so often a question—the rhythm of trains, of art, of language—is not the simple temporal harmony of parts extraneous to each other. It is rather a profound interrelation affecting the parts internally, altering their nature. Thus the comparison with chemistry.

When, in an essay called "Le Principe d'utilité," Cendrars abounds in praise for the engineers of the epoch, the manner in which he is able to identify exterior physical constructions with the internal mental impulses and their verbal and plastic expression becomes clear. He compares the material of hardened steels, sharp-edged glass, nickel, and copper to currents of high-tension ideas, and the geometrical progress of inventions, the brightly-colored posters which replace the strict formal categories of flowerbeds, to a new writing, a "verbe coloré" to match the multicolored life of the poet and, ideally, of the people. His rejection of those flowerbeds (representing a restricted vision of time and space) for the image of the whirlwind enables him to absorb, in a further spiral, the least "poetic" elements into his writing. His *Poèmes élastiques* extend to include not only quotations from prose ("vous vous imaginiez monsieur Barzum, que j'allais tranquillement vous permettre de ruiner mes projets, de livrer ma fille à la justice, vous aviez pensé cela?"/you imagined, Mr. Barzum, that I was just going to let you ruin my plans, turn my daughter in, you thought that?—from *I*, 100)[7a] but also a description of the *outside* of a volume, as if the most exterior ideas were to be easily taken into the inside of poetic language ("Paris au Dépôt de la Librairie, 1835, 4 vol. in-16 jésus"—from *I*, 100). As the concept of the purely mechanical is superseded by the profound alternations of the chemical, so Cendrars here goes beyond the simplest notion of collage or montage (the process which he admires above all in the films of Griffith and according to which a number of his novels would be written) to that of the elastic poem. The structure itself stretches, while remaining a unit; the points or stages of the apparently discontinuous stretch into a

[7a] The name suggests Henri-Martin Barzun, creator of Dramatism, a theory which included simultaneous recitations or Simultanism as its final stage. The changed letter n/m permits ambiguity.

continuous surface, whose shape and size thus vary at the various moments of the text.

"Aux 5 coins," one of the elastic poems, gives the best possible description of "today's poetry" in its clarity, its mobile brilliance, and its explosive power:

Oser et faire du bruit
Tout est couleur mouvement explosion lumière

(Be daring and make noise
All is color movement explosion light)

and in the relation between the universe of light and the poet's expression of it (the accent on the mouth and language here reminding us of Apollinaire):

La vie fleurit aux fenêtres du soleil[8]
Qui se fond dans ma bouche

. . .

Bouche d'or
La poésie est en jeu. (I, 98)

(Life flowers at the sun's windows
Melting in my mouth

. . .

Golden mouth
Poetry is at stake)[9]

[8] Michel Butor, in his "Monument de rien pour Apollinaire" (*Répertoire III*, Gallimard, 1968), makes a detailed study—formal and thematic—of the idea of windows in the poetry of Apollinaire and its connection with the simultaneous theories and paintings of Delaunay. Pierre Francastel, in his introduction to Delaunay's previously unpublished writings and conversations (Robert Delaunay, *Du Cubisme à l'art abstrait* [S.E.V.P.E.N., 1957]), traces the progression of the artist's subjects from tow-

ers to towns to windows to the circular forms of disks, the sun, and the helix. As Cendrars' use of the window is intimately connected to Delaunay's painting and theory, so his use of the spiral form is probably connected to Delaunay's circular forms—in particular, the helix. They share the "esthétique simultanée" (p. 184), participating together in the "univers simultanique." (p. 181) And while the initial theory of simultaneous representation may have led to static portrayals of differing perspectives seen at once (thence Apollinaire's association of Delaunay with the cubists), Delaunay himself went on, after 1913, to another point of view, from which motion mattered above all, not the actual motion of objects but that conferred on them by the play of light: "Un *mouvement* qui fait naître le sujet." (p. 168) "Tout est couleur en mouvement (profondeur): qui est la construction de ce que j'appelle la représentation simultanée." (p. 184)

Delaunay's own commentary on the "Prose du Transsibérien" accentuates the qualities of motion and of freedom, judging these to be the essential characteristics of synchronic or simultaneous representation. The poem gives free rein to "la sensibilité de substituer un ou plusieurs mots, un mouvement de mots, ce qui forme la forme, la vie du poème, le simultanisme." (p. 112)

For the confused relations between the Italian futurists and the notions of cubism, Orphism, and simultanism, see L. C. Breunig's edition of Apollinaire, *Chroniques d'art* (Gallimard, 1960), Pär Bergman's "*Modernolatria*" *et* "*Simultanéità*" (Bonniers, 1962), Francis Steegmuller's *Apollinaire: Poet Among the Painters* (Farrar, Straus, 1963), and Marianne W. Martin, *Futurist Art and Theory* (Clarendon Press, 1968), in the last of which we are reminded in the appendix that according to Severini, Apollinaire would have conferred the title "futurist" on all manifestations of modernity in art had not Marinetti objected to his use of the term, and that Apollinaire was eventually to accuse Delaunay of appropriating the term and the notion of simultaneity from the Italian futurists without giving them due credit. And, for a commentary on Delaunay's painting as, in his own words, "windows by simultaneous contrast," see Roger Shattuck, *The Banquet Years: The Arts in France 1884-1918* (Harcourt, Brace, 1955), where there is a clear discussion of Apollinaire's calligrammatic form and a description of simultanist poetry as the opposite of simple narration, relying on a sort of *découpage poétique*: "It represents an effort to retain a moment of experience without sacrificing its logically unrelated variety. In poetry it also means an effort to neutralize the passage of time involved in the act of reading. The fragments of a poem are deliberately kept in a random order to be reassembled in a single instant of consciousness. An unusual typographical image on the page can help suggest this instantaneous experience and dissipate the temporal act of reading. Simultanism means a telescoping of time, a poetic technique that achieves the opposite effect from the regulated flow of music." (p. 238)

The Bergman study is, as its title indicates, of particular interest for the present discussion. After an introduction on the myth of the modern and a description of Italian futurism in its attachment to the goddess *Velocità* and to the three related notions of "anti-passatismo, dinamismo, attivismo," he analyzes the difference between Italian futurism, where simultaneity is useful for transcribing the modern world (Boccioni: "la simultanéità degli stati d'animo") and Delaunay's more strictly aesthetic concern with the idea ("la simultanéité dans le contraste des couleurs"). Delaunay disapproved of futurist simultaneity of the kind represented in the famous "Dog on a Leash," where the many legs pictured at once were supposed to describe movement. As for the quarrel about the term itself, Delaunay borrowed it after the futurist exhibition in Paris of 1912, but, on the other hand, the Italian futurists concentrated on the simultaneous contrast only after Delaunay's "fenêtres simultanées" and his "disques simultanées" (based on Chevreul's discovery of the "loi du contraste des couleurs complémentaires"); see Bergman, pp. 263-74.

Some of the statements quoted from Delaunay in this book are remarkably similar in tone and vocabulary to Cendrars' sentences on depth: for example, on p. 269, "tout est couleur par contraste, tout est couleur en mouvement, tout est profondeur" or "il y a *simultanéité*, c'est-à-dire *profondeur*. Nous voyons jusqu'aux étoiles." The last sentence reappears verbatim in Cendrars, as do many other direct quotations, in a brilliant and effective collage. Bergman's commentary on Cendrars' *ubiquist* imagination and its relations to simultaneity and contrast in art is clearly the fullest and most valid available. Entitled *"Le Premier livre simultané* et d'autres poèmes d'avant-guerre de Blaise Cendrars," it begins with the poet's announcement: "J'ai la fièvre. Et c'est pourquoi j'aime la peinture des Delaunay, pleine de soleil,

The accent placed on the simultaneous gesture is in itself a protest against the narrow and the linear, as the accent, borrowed from Delaunay, put on the *simultaneous contrast,* is a protest against the facility and the narrow range of the simple contrast (of black and white, for instance). "The simultaneous contrast is depth perceived. Reality. Form. Construction. Representation." (*A,* 128); or again: "Disk. Rhythm. Dance. A color orange and a color violet devour each other." (*A,* 14) Founded in the resemblance between things as much as in their basic difference, this kind of contrast accentuates the continuous above the discontinuous. All the stages of a journey are linked and yet separate; their cohesion is assured by the movement of the voyager.

---

de ruts, de violences" (from "La Prose du Transsibérien," *Der Sturm,* Nov. 1913, nos. 184-85, p. 121) and continues with a sketch of the varied sorts of contrast in the "Prose," which was, together with Sonia Delaunay's illustrations in mostly circular form, the First Simultaneous Book. He enumerates contrasts in time and feeling (Jehanne as Jeanne d'Arc and as little Jeanne, martyr and whore), contrasts of words and images (such as the line "Et je construirai un hangar pour mon avion avec les os fossiles de mammouth" or "Et nous nous aimerons bien bourgeoisement près du pôle"), and contrasts of legend and reality (Ali Baba set against the specialists of international express trains). We also find references to cinematography (the windows of the train compartment resembling the movie screen, a poetic *découpage* resembling the film cutting of American Westerns such as Porter's), on telegraphy (the Télégraphie Sans Fil like Marinetti's "Immaginazione senza fili"), on newspaper headline style, and a convincing list of relationships between specific poems and specific painters.

[9] This should be read *simultaneously* as "Poetry is in play" and "Poetry is at stake."

This theory is the basis for Cendrars' admiration of the cinema,[10] a medium effective precisely because the simultaneous levels and perspectives involve the onlooker, now become active: "The spectator who is no longer immobile in his seat, who is snatched up, roughed up, participating in the action, seeing himself on the screen among the crowd's convulsions. . . ." (*A*, 65) His involvement is paralleled by that of the camera itself, as it moves to register the sections of reality it joins and to create the new unity deeper than the partial links we observe with our more limited vision.

As an experiment in the contrast of the pictorial and the cinematic, we might briefly compare (or make a simultaneous contrast of passages from) a still-life poem of 1914 for the artist de la Fresnaye ("Natures mortes") and a poem of 1916 on a child's play war, "La Guerre au Luxembourg." The distance between these poems, from the first, showing a linear pictoriality, to the second and more cinematic one, may be seen as merely formal, or as indicative of a change in vision. In the first, the colors of the painting are placed, in italics and unattached as to gender, among the objects to which they apply, so that they are at once separated from them and closely associated with them:

Et la table de l'architecte
Est ainsi strictment belle

[10] Its greatness lies in the surprises it offers, but even these are due less to differences than to resemblances, to the "correspondances entre l'irréfléchi, l'inerte, l'indéchiffrable, l'informe, l'informulé" (*Trop c'est trop* [Denoël, 1957], p. 191).

40

Noir
Avec une bouteille d'encre de Chine
Et des chemises bleues
Bleu
Rouge
Puis il y a aussi un litre, un litre de sensualité
Et cette haute nouveauté
Blanc
Des feuilles de papier blanc (*I*, 98)

(And the architect's table
Is thus of real beauty
Black
With a bottle of India ink
And blue shirts
Blue
Red
And there is a liter too, a liter of sensuality
And this latest trick
White
Pages of white paper)

The colors stand out from the objects, then, so that the painted *language* is directly in contact with the colored canvas without any necessary mediation of the actual *objects*. And yet it is a genuine still life, containing the typical cubist objects to which we are accustomed, in typical simple cylindrical and rectangular shapes: the table and the paper contrasting with the bottles of ink and wine ("litre de sensualité"), the colors standing next to the objects they define, leaving no place for surprise.

41

In the second poem, however, the form and the mood are completely different. Here the right-hand margin supplies a simultaneous voice across the space of the page. A child's game of war in the gardens is described in a sequence of catalogued items, and loud statements on the left (a gun, shouts of high-pitched voices) are paralleled on the right by an actual description of the words shouted ("Moi!" "Moi!" "Moi!", childish and self-centered). A parade where disabled soldiers pass in the left margin is simultaneously compared and contrasted with the passing of the flag on the right ("Rouge Blanc Bleu"). The closing of the garden is set across from the slow rhythm of the word RÊVEURS, as it stretches, one letter at a time, down the page, descriptive of the mood of the children and the garden, of the separation and of the twilight. Finally, an actual landscape described in two lines is echoed by an evocation of "La Mer," in capital letters on the right as it is symbolic of the distance, and then that evocation is echoed on the left in small letters, where it is discussed in the flat tones of the everyday ("Et peut-être bien la mer."). The interest here lies not just in the two simple and simultaneous readings on the horizontal and vertical lines—but also in the fact that the reading can be done in many directions, as if in a spiral: left to right, right to left, horizontally, diagonally, vertically. For example, we might take the passage centered on the parade:

Puis on relève les morts
Tout le monde veut en être
Ou tout au moins blessé   ROUGE

Coupe coupe
Coupe le bras coupe la tête   BLANC
On donne tout
Croix-Rouge   BLEU
Les infirmières en bas (*I*, 112)

(Then they pick up the dead bodies
Everyone wants to be one of those
Or wounded at the very least   RED
Cut cut
Cut the arms off cut the head off   WHITE
We give everything
Red Cross   BLUE
The nurses downstairs)

Here, in the symbolic parade on the right and the actual one on the left, the large RED repeats the color of the wound on the left and leads to the macabre "Coupe coupe," while on the right it represents the patriotic, if slightly foolish ideal of the onlookers who would just as soon be sufferers; the WHITE makes an echo for the implied consequence of the cutting, "bled white," and leads to the verbal image of sacrifice identical with that English expression (having given everything, one has been bled white); now the red of Croix-Rouge takes up again the initial color of the passing flag and leads to its opposite, BLUE, and then, diagonally to the color of the nurses' uniform. The cycle RED WHITE BLUE is preserved on the "realistic" and the symbolic level, as well as on the visual/verbal one. Any idea of the still life has been left behind, as the progression of the poem forces a simultaneous mental movement beyond the linear reading and picturesque visual coloration. The poetic gesture here expressed is the equivalent of cinema and the voyage; the reader must cooperate in the poem *and* in the vision, unless he chooses to reject both.

3. THE NAKED GESTURE

A last indication, if one is needed, that Cendrars is more concerned with motion than with spectacle is his emphasis on the *dépouillement* of the gesture. Stripped bare of any adjectives which would serve as mere ornaments, it functions, whatever its purpose, in simple activity, unhindered by trivial detail. Another "elastic" poem, "La Tête," begins with the gruesome transformed into the serious:

> La guillotine est le chef-d'oeuvre de l'art plastique
> Son déclic
> Crée le mouvement perpétuel (*I*, 103)[11]

> (The guillotine is the masterpiece of plastic art
> Its click
> Creates perpetual motion)

It ends in praise of Archipenko's egg-shaped sculpture, whose bare perspectives are devoid even of color, an ascetic parallel simultaneous with the "verbe coloré":

[11] This part of the poem, around which the rest is built—or to which it is added—occurs already in "Le Panama ou les aventures de mes sept oncles," I, 58. In the *Inédits*, we find a "Dialogue sur la sculpture" of June, 1914; here Cendrars cites an interview with a friend who says, "Ce que je pense de la sculpture? Le chef d'oeuvre de la sculpture moderne est la guillotine: son déclic crée le mouvement perpétuel."

Maintenu en équilibre intense
Comme une toupie immobile
Sur sa pointe animée
Vitesse
Il se dépouille
Des ondes multicolores
Des zones de couleur
Et tourne dans la profondeur
Nu.
Neuf.
Total.

(Held in intense balance
Like a motionless top
On its animated point
Rapidity
It strips itself bare
Of multicolored waves
Of colored zones
And whirls in the depths
Naked.
New.
Total.

The immobile matched to the mobile,[12] purity matched to profundity and novelty, the spiral matched to the simple, both the sculpture and the poem identified with it are perfect and complete. A full stop after each of the

[12] A later image of the mobile matched to the immobile is equally impressive, that is, the description in one of the "Feuilles de route" of the wake of the ship as it makes "un grand arc de cercle miroitant sur la mer immobile," II, 47.

three final descriptions marks them also as completely sufficient, in spite of their brevity.

In fact Cendrars never loses his awareness of the gesture of writing, often alluding to it, shaping even some of the rapid travel sketches (or "Feuilles de route") around it: "Mes journées seront bien remplies/ Je n'ai pas une minute à perdre/ J'écris" (*II*, 68); ". . . je redescends dans ma cabine/ Et me remets au travail" (*II*, 70); "J'ai voilé le miroir de l'armoire à glace pour ne pas me voir écrire" (*II*, 71); "J'étouffe et j'écris j'écris" (*II*, 80); "POURQUOI J'ECRIS? Parce que. . . ." (*II*, 90) Yet he pretends never to have attributed to that gesture any exaggerated importance—like the loss of his arm, the 36 professions he claims to have exercised,[13] or his diverse kinds of exploit, it is simply one of the given points to be mentioned and then superseded in the process of moving about. It is the *continuous gesture* which is significant, the cinema which takes precedence over still photographs. To his poems he gives the simple titles of "poèmes dépouillés," "poème-télégramme," "poème-océan,"[14] "cartes postales." Like the bright and

[13] *Histoires vraies* (Grasset, 1938), p. 220.

[14] Apollinaire describes the *design* of his own *Lettre-Océan* thus: ". . . dans la *Lettre-Océan* ce qui s'impose et l'emporte, c'est l'aspect typographique, précisément l'image, soit le dessin. Que cette image soit composée de fragments parlés, il n'importe *psychologiquement*, car le lien entre ces fragments n'est plus celui de la logique grammaticale, mais celui d'une logique idéographique aboutissant à un ordre de disposition spatiale tout contraire à celui de la juxtaposition discursive. . . ." Quoted in Michel Butor, *Répertoire II* (Editions de Minuit, 1964), p. 120.

One of the more interesting and less frequently noticed links between Cendrars and Apollinaire is their attitude toward the cinema. For both poets, it is the ideal medium for the *epic* con-

bare posters, simple headlines or titles are quite as valuable as what they might announce. A poem called "Titres" describes the limited outline of the new spirit, completely unconcerned with the picturesque, more forceful as it is less complicated.

Formes sueurs chevelures
Le bond d'être
Depouillé
Premier poème sans métaphores
Sans images
Nouvelles
L'esprit nouveau (*I*, 101)

(Forms perspirations heads of hair
The leap of being
Bare
First poem without metaphors
Without new
Images
The new spirit)

Writing is not living, Cendrars repeats. It should not therefore be given a greater importance than it deserves.

In 1929, Cendrars finally abandoned, consciously, the genre of poetry for that of the novel, because even the transcription of voyage seems immobile. "Only the nov-

---

ception, because of its possible scope and because of its universal popularity. Apollinaire likens the projectionist to a medieval *jongleur*, binding the spectators or audience with the inescapable spell of heroic narration and larger-than-life spectacle. (It is no less interesting, in relation to some of the other chapters, to note Apollinaire's idea of a *circus theatre*, an idea stressing once more the simultaneous vision.)

elistic formula allows the development of the *active character* of events and contemporary personages who do not really assume their proper importance except in *motion.*" (*A*, 94) The notion of *gigantisme*, the essentially grandiose character necessary in the cinema, colors his conception of plastic art as well as verbal art. (But the large canvas requires an actual subject, says Cendrars, thus rejecting altogether our abstract art done large.) As befits the concept of magnitude, Cendrars' own sentences either are lengthy or are made up of brief moments, separated by periods; they are joined, in principle, by the eye acting as movie camera.

Here again, however, there is to be no allowance made for heroics. His novels, often great in scope, are still punctuated by the poetic *JE* he finds absent from the works of his contemporaries, where, he says, "The poetic *I* is proscribed." (*I*, 245) But the gestures attributed to this self or to any other personage, although they are carefully observed, are not deliberately aggrandized in any way. Rather the contrary, for a sort of final reduction often takes place: many of the gestures in the poems and novels stop with the indefinite word "etc.," and the project for the film "La Fin du monde, filmée par l'ange Notre-Dame" ends "ETC."[15] There is no point in going further than one needs, in accumulating useless details or exaggerating normal actions. In a collection of essays with the title of *Trop c'est trop*, significant in this context, Cendrars mocks the larger-than-life action of epic heroes, and of fictional heroes, by the simple interrupted sentence, where the end trails off

[15] Seghers, 1949, p. 61.

48

into nothing after a beginning which would ordinarily indicate grandeur of action, and the scope and tone of the universal:

C'est une épopée . . .
Un héros . . .
Chacun se vante . . .
On raconte autour du feu . . .[16]

(It's an epic . . .
A hero . . .
Each one brags . . .
Telling stories around the fire . . .)

In each sentence above, the large-scale beginning is too unspecific to convince us of any real epic content; otherwise, the open end might be felt as the celebration of all possible events which the opening had conceivably prepared for (a frequent and generally successful technique of several surrealist authors). It is rather an intended vagueness, leading nowhere, whose very lack of direction and end has a negative effect on the starting point itself. This stylistic device is in fact the startling opposite of the poet's bare and admiring salute to the modern gesture, where the elements are closed and complete in themselves:

Nu.
Neuf.
Total.

At the same time, the homesickness suffered by one of the Seven Uncles in the poem "Le Panama," the re-

[16] *Op. cit.*, p. 93.

gret, fear, and tedium recurring along with the continual passion for travel ("Je voudrais/ Je voudrais n'avoir jamais fait mes voyages"—*I*, 45), the possibility of suicide on which Cendrars meditates out of the fullness of living, as he explains it—these *simultaneous* contrasts suffice to remove from the series of epic voyages the stigma of exaggeration without affecting the significance of the adventurous intention. And even if the real scope of action is limited, by a formal or mental reversing of the spiral, a series of the same voyages or same actions repeated can open out infinitely, proving that the exterior and occasionally involuntary bareness (*dépouillement*) of the gesture, of the landscape, or of the poem has no effect on the interior depth: "The writer given to frequent meditations on his past self, as I am, never climbs the same staircase, never goes down in the same cellar, is never at the top of the same tower; he is instead always discovering something new. . . ."[17]

But does not this constant reference to the act of writing, to the novel character of one's own poems, or to their intrinsically mobile nature, spotlight that act, arresting the attention of the spectator and even that of the actor himself? Ideally, the will to motion would determine a gesture continuous and cinematic, pointing to a place beyond its own self-consciousness: in practice, however, the author's concentration on his gesture may impede the *passage*. The problem recurs in all the authors discussed except Benjamin Péret, who may be said, for that very reason, to make the only genuine epic gesture in the sense we attribute to it here: a continu-

[17] *Blaise Cendrars vous parle, op. cit.*, p. 103.

ous sweep of mobility sufficiently unself-conscious never to betray its own movement by the complacency or the anguish of a gaze turned upon itself.

B. *Tristan Tzara: The Circus of Language*

ET LE LARGE SON DE LA
VITESSE EST LENTEUR FIXÉE
DANS LES CADRES DE L'HORIZON
"Bois parlant ou intelligible
signe de l'Ile des Pâques,"
De nos oiseaux

1. MANIFESTATION AND MIRAGE

The direct opposite of nostalgia, the antisentimental action of Dada is the present made manifest. Dada or "Dada/Tzara" rejects sentiment as a diluting agent, or as a brake retarding the possible speed of the poetic gesture.

"Let everyone shout"; "Every page must explode"; "Watch out!"[1] It is not necessary to fire on the first passerby; as Mr. Aa the antiphilosopher explains, the least significant gesture is already an attack. Writing, of all gestures possibly the least significant, falls directly into this category as a profoundly antisocial undertaking: "Every act is a mental gunshot . . . and with the words set down on paper, I enter solemnly toward myself." (*SMD*, 49) Language—Dada language—is a brutal attack on the outer world of reality and sameness of per-

[1] *Sept manifestes dada, suivis de lampisteries* (Pauvert, 1963), pp. 32, 26, 63. (Hereafter referred to as *SMD*.)

ception common to the non-Dadas. Tzara calls this dull community of vision a fat and lazy objectivity, taking, of course, every available occasion to destroy its placid assurance with subversive (subjective) manifestations.

Dada praises the IDIOT as the *antiman* precisely because his language is free from the assumptions and associations normal men make by habit or logic. Dada attacks the bankers of language, who believe in words and their accumulated meanings as if they were precious (and negotiable), calling its own communications a mere "chat" in order to discourage speculators. Dada recommends a deliberate leveling of human instincts as a necessary negative step toward the removal of exterior *interest*: the invoking of chance in Dada poetry is a protest against the rich productions of craftsmanship and of autobiographical revelation. Language has been a utopia, a paradise of certain value. Now it will be a spectacular disavowal of its own worth, a permanent manifesto of voluntary self-destruction and self-impoverishment, deriving its authority from its severity.

All statements and all manifestos will be undermined as they are made—"No more words!" (*SMD*, 47) cries the Dadaist, and continues to talk. "DADA—exists in order to lie," (*SMD*, 73) and in fact Dada does. By the end of the sentence, the beginning has been disproved: "Watch out! Now is the time to tell you that I lied. That is to say I am lying now . . . I am lying while I write that I am lying because I am not lying. . . ." (*SMD*, 50) To finish or make comprehensible any sentence is "the bitterest act of a bandit," (*SMD*, 50) an antihuman mirage, mechanical, dishonest, ridiculous.

Inconsistency is to be cherished above all, the mirage is valued like the lie. "We are not simple," (*SMD*, 17) and yet Dada is supposed to be simplicity in action. "Is simplicity simple or dada?" (*SMD*, 57) Dada gesture calls for an initial simple spontaneity, free of description, quick-moving, cosmic: "La simplicité active." (*SMD*, 29) Dada's language cannot describe Dada action for those who are not participants in it. It has no obligations either to the actual state of things nor to those who might have an interest in that actuality, nor even to the subversive theatre it represents. Dada speaks violently against the real, against *others*, and against itself; the Dada gesture starts from the absolute denial of any common basis in human mentality or perception, of any community of believers, even in Dada. Any Dada work is the interior transposition of a highly individual personality (an auto-kleptomaniac, says Tzara), whose language cannot operate under logical exterior norms. Dada performances and manifestations may appear to be addressed to the spectators; at their noisiest moment, however, Tzara yells: "No more onlookers!" (*SMD*, 47) Dada is a pure art which refuses to be judged on its façade, a pure language and pure spectacle which leaves its listeners and its spectators behind, on the surface which the speaker or performer has already deserted and which disintegrates after him.

The most violent gesture is in this case mental: the subversion of our faith in theatre as theatre and its language as language. We watch an action without meaning for us, all the more spectacular for its non-significance.

2. A POETRY OF MOTION, VISION, AND COHERENCE

"Dada is a quantity of life in transparent transformation, effortless and gyrating."[2] Tzara's description of the universe of Dada denies progress for pure movement, and deliberate form for spontaneous vitality. Neither his often-quoted formula for constructing a Dada poem (cut out the words in a newspaper article of the desired length, shake them in a bag, remove them in random order), nor his superb example of a poem constructed in this way ("prix ils sont hier convenant ensuite tableaux . . ."/ price they are yesterday fitting then paintings . . .) contradicts this vision of easy energy; nor can they be said to arouse, in general, any overwhelming passion for the prolonged reading of much Dada poetry.[3]

[2] *Ibid.*, p. 69.

[3] The peculiar fashion in which the poems were published reflects a fortuitousness worthy of Dada. Since the edition of 1918 is printed in a narrow column, it is impossible to tell which lines are continuations of the preceding ones and which are meant to be new; unfortunately, the most recent edition (1946), which has a wide column of print, takes the 1918 edition for a model instead of going back to the manuscript. Consequently, many lines which were originally long and made a definite contrast in texture when combined with the far shorter ones are chopped up into two, three, or even four lines, resulting in a final impression of jerkiness often not present in the original manuscript. There are also other deformations: part of a poem placed in another poem (see the last of the *Vingt-cinq-et-un poèmes*, "le sel et le vin," whose first line comes from one page and the remaining part from the other side of the page, leaving the rest of the first page to be part of "la grande complainte de mon obscurité deux"), and so on. Parts of lines are somehow lost in the transition between manuscript and printing, to say nothing

But if this poetry is indeed a chance conglomeration of phrases, what can explain Tzara's statement that the Dada poem is the quintessence of pure structure, that it is based on a rhythm both unheard and unseen which he calls the "light of an interior grouping beamed toward a constellation of order"? (*SMD*, 106) Is this a genuine conviction, or a supreme example of the Dada joke? And if we consider the statement a serious one, we still do not know if the innate coherence is in each case due to the constants in the poet's own personality somehow reflected in the poem, or if it originates within the being of the poem itself. (Of course, since ambivalence and ambiguity are essential to Dada and to the extremes of its character, we should not wish for clarification or resolution.)

There remains a more significant problem: since the essential groupings are intuitive and interior, is it not as in the case of the Dada theatre a useless enterprise to examine the necessarily partial and exterior links perceived by the reader, since they may lie in an entirely different realm from the ones inside? Perhaps so; but perhaps also the still frequent assumption that Dada was a totally negative and incoherent attitude which produced totally negative and incoherent results suffices to justify the brief catalogue of a few surface indica-

---

of the rearrangements. Perhaps this does not matter, if one considers only Tzara's purely negative statements about art, so much more famous than his positive ones about poetry. But since he intended his *Note sur la poésie*, quoted here, to be a sort of preface to this work, it seems valid to take the statements within it as serious, at least in a Dada framework.

tions of poetic coherence, whether or not they have any apparent relevance to the interior ordering, and whether we consider them artifacts left by chance or predictive markers set up on purpose.[4]

Even Tzara's earliest French poems,[5] the *Vingt-cinq poèmes dada* of 1918, show a certain unity of mood and imagery. For instance, the poem "Printemps" begins with the morbid instruction,

placer l'enfant dans le vase au fond de minuit
  et la plaie[6]

(place the child in the vase at the depth of midnight
  and the wound),

and continues with images of stagnation, melancholy, imprisonment, exile, and attempts at escape. Many of these images are attributed to animals: unhealthy water trickles down the antelope's legs, while the caged peacock is thirsty; broken grasshoppers and ant hearts are sown in the garden, while the deer flee over the sharp points of black branches. The title seems ironic in the most obvious and least subtle sense, since spring is rarely associated with melancholy, either in the human or in the natural world.

"Petite ville en Sibérie," from the same collection, be-

[4] They could of course be both, since chance and will meet so often in the Dada and the surrealist universes.

[5] His Roumanian poems of 1912-15 are not in question here since they are "pre-Dada," although it must be admitted that Tzara himself refused any such distinctions as "pre-Dada." See Claude Sernet's introduction to and translations of Tristan Tzara, *Les Premiers poèmes* (Seghers, 1965).

[6] In Tristan Tzara, *Morceaux choisis* (Bordas, 1947), p. 31. (Hereafter referred to as *MC*.)

56

gins with three parallel motionless and one-dimensional images which utterly negate any joy or freedom (people flattened together on the ceiling in a blue light, signs pasted on doors, and a label stuck on a medicine bottle) and continues with a series of alternating images of order or static positions and rapid, irrational, or frenzied movement, at times actual and at times only dreamed of (both sets of images stressed here):

c'est la maison CALME mon ami *tremble*
et puis la *danse* LOURDE courbée
offre la VIEILLESSE *sautillant* d'heure en heure
    sur le CADRAN
le collier INTACT des lampes de *locomotives*
    coupées descend quelquefois parmi nous
et *se dégonfle* tu nommes cela SILENCE . . . et mon
    coeur *décent* sur des maisons basses plus
    basses *plus hautes plus basses* sur lesquelles
    je veux *galoper* . . . DORMIR oh oui si l'on
    pouvait seulement
le *train* de nouveau . . . je RESTE sur le banc
. . .

des coeurs et des yeux *roulent* dans ma bouche
en marche (*MC*, 32)

(it's the CALM house *tremble* my friend
and then the HEAVY curved *dance*
shows us AGE *leaping about* from hour to hour
    on the CLOCKFACE
the WHOLE necklace of *cut-off locomotive lamps*
    descends among us sometimes
and *deflates* you call that SILENCE . . . and my

decent heart *descends* on houses *lower lower*
still higher still lower over which I'd like to
gallop . . . to SLEEP oh yes if only one could
the *train* again . . . I STAY SEATED on the bench
. . .
hearts and eyes *roll about* in my mouth
on the march)

In spite of the tranquil light cast by a herring tin on the
tin roofs, our final picture of the "Petite Ville" includes
little children in pools of blood and a bitter image of
frantic motion in its complete futility:

courons plus vite encore
toujours partout nous resterons entre des fenêtres
noires (*MC*, 32)

(let's run still more quickly
always everywhere we'll be trapped between black
windows)

The poem has thus progressed from imprisonment in a
blue light, through the total inability either to move as
one would like or to rest, to a final permanent confine-
ment within an absence of light and vision.

Some of these poems are based on contrasting images
of motion and immobility like those just mentioned but
show, instead of any sustained atmosphere, certain
shifts of mood parallel to the shifts of images. "Gare,"
another of the *Vingt-cinq poèmes dada*, opens with a
conscious separation between action and noise on one
hand and the passive indifference of the poet on the
other: "danse crie casse/ roule j'attends sur le banc"

(*MC*, 33) (dance shout break/ roll I am waiting on the bench.) Then follows an ironic comparison between the vital world of nature and the sheltered human world:

Le vol d'un oiseau qui brûle
est ma force virile sous la coupole
je cherche asile (*MC*, 33)

(the flight of a burning bird
is my manly strength under the cupola
I seek shelter)

Echoing this last image are three examples of the poet's face enclosed—first by the circle of evening, then by a suitcase, and finally by the bars of a cage. Like the title image of the station, the strange conception of the face in the suitcase implies both motion (departure) and spatial limit. The suitcase has a logical place in the poem, for shortly after a question as to his possible action ("partir"), the poet, who has been quietly reading on the bench in the evening, answers immediately in the affirmative: "je pars ce soir." The evening calm is spoiled in any case by dogs and jaguars howling in a factory but also in the poet's bed, a final image of rest denied which reminds us of the preceding poem's "dormir oh oui si l'on pouvait seulement." Most of the other elements in "Gare" reflect either the peaceful atmosphere with which the poet initially surrounds himself (his silent reading of the paper, the precise and wise god, an orderly friendship, the listening light near the beginning, and the spherical glimmers at the end) or the shattering of it (the poet's blackened eyes that he hurls into the waterfall, the weeping spark, and the lions and clowns in the last line, directly related to the dogs and jaguars, which close the poem on the mocking and shrilly active tone of a circus).

"Les Saltimbanques" (where the image of the circus performer mentioned in "Gare" is repeated) revolves about the whining sound of an accordion ("glwawawa") and its obvious rhythm:

> les cerveaux se gonflent s'aplatissent des
> ballons lourds s'épuisent s'aplatissent
> . . .
> se gonflent s'aplatissent se gonflent s'aplatissent
> s'aplatissent (*MC*, 76)

> (the brains swell up flatten out heavy balloons
> wear out flatten out
> . . .
> swell up flatten out swell up flatten out
> flatten out).

The poem is arranged on the page to suggest movement and variations in volume, but Tzara inserts an absolute contrast to the movement, characteristically self-referential:

> NTOUCA qui saute
> marotte
> qui est dada qui est DADA
> le poème statique est une nouvelle invention
> (*MC*, 76)[7]

[7] From *De nos oiseaux* (Kra, 1923). Before publication, the poet eliminated here the following lines in the proofs of this

(NTOUCA leaping
    silly doll
which is dada which is DADA
the static poem is a new invention)

Dada poetry is of course anything but static. In fact, the reason the poet must reject all sentimentality in his work, according to Tzara, is that the "humidity" of tears often visible in past art might retard this intensely modern dynamism, merciless and severe. The ideal Dada poem "shoves or digs a crater, is silent, murders or shrieks along accelerated speeds." (*SMD*, 105)

One of the basic tensions in Tzara's early poetry results from the frequent juxtaposition of motion with the formal stability of certain geometrical figures. In "Gare," a poem set within a railway station, the flight of a bird is compared to the poet's search for refuge in the circular safety of a *cupola* (the dome above the waiting room); his invocation of a possible departure and his resolution to leave are separated only by the image of his (round) face in the *circle* of evening. As the circus performer climbs up the ladder, in a transposition of images of risk, his "oblong" skull makes a sharp contrast—although the vision is only implied—to the repeated *rectangles* of the ladder formed by the rungs.

---

poem, simplifying for intensity and, for the same reason, eliminating the marks of juncture ("avec") to leave only the striking juxtaposition ("mboco H₂S"). The original conception was quite different in feeling, more balanced and of a slower rhythm:

quand mbengo est en équilibre avec tritrilôulo
mboco avec H₂S
10054 avec nkogunlda
nwega anami avec koutimpoco avec moumbimba

Finally, the hearts of medicinal plants are opened to become *spheroid*-shaped lights, echoing in a modified form the shape of the circus *ring*.

In "Circuit total par la lune et par la couleur," a poem entirely about motion and circling, as its title indicates, the *circular* and *oval* forms predominate. The announced image of the moon is followed in rapid succession by an iron eye, then by portholes, olives swelling up into symmetric crystallizations (with the noise "pac pac"), a lemon, a coin, kiosks, and the sun. And at the same time, all the nervous dancing of the Dada god, the *vertical* flight of butterflies and of rivers, the *linear* motion implied by roads and the diagonals of rains, the *elongating* of bridges stand in opposition to the circular forms. This series of balanced and opposed images, together with the dilating of cells, the writhing of yellow snakes, and the rapid march of all the shades of the color red, are subject to the sudden miraculous arrangements omnipresent in the infinitely mobile universe of Dada spontaneity, where there is nevertheless a strong accent on the order of the spectacle. Light beams range themselves around magnetic poles like peacock feathers spread out, waterfalls gather by groups in their own light—each thing is ordered, it appears, by its own particular laws—while the sun itself is slowly unfolded by an enormous peacock at the North Pole: poles and peacocks repeated in an ordering of images. Even the poet shows some surprise at the spectacular arrangement:

quand je demande comment
les fosses hurlent
seigneur ma géométrie (*MC*, p. 74)

(when I ask how
the ditches shriek
lord my geometry)

In his "Note sur la poésie," Tzara demands that the
Dada poet write with a joyous rapidity, enthusiasm,
and intensity, that he present a constantly varied spectacle: "Flow in all colors . . ."; (*SMD*, 104) his own
poetry is as diverse and as brightly colored as Benjamin
Péret's poems and stories, and it communicates the
same peculiarly visual directness. The peacock feathers
and the northern lights ("la nuit des couleurs") of the
"Circuit . . . par la couleur" have counterparts in many
other early poems, where the incessant transformations
are sometimes rhythmic, but appeal more often and
more vividly to the sight. Still another circus poem, "Le
Dompteur de lions se souvient," insists on the immediate attention of the onlooker, who will later be called
upon to participate in the world of spectacle,

regarde-moi et sois couleur
plus tard (*MC*, p. 30)

(look at me and be color
later),

and then presents a garishly tinted assortment of blue
antelopes, a red so vivid that it rolls of its own momentum with no less energy than do the marching reds already mentioned ("roule roule rouge"), and a green
horse, with a number of white parasols for contrast. No
Dada reader would have expected a subtle watercolor,
since he knows that "Dada has abolished all nuances."

(*SMD*, p. 119) Dada colors must have the clarity and pure affirmation of the glass corridors and the mountains of crystal which are the true domain of the Dada artist.

Tzara often associates the extreme brilliance of his colors with height, in a further denial of the ordinary drab furnishings and undramatic spectacle of our normal world, located at eye-level:

le jet d'eau s'échappe et monte
vers les autres couleurs[8]

en arc-en-ciel de cendre
les couleurs humides rodent
ivres[9]

salis mouillés lambeaux de nuit nous avons élevé
en nous chacun de nous une tour de couleur si
   hautaine

[8] "La Grande Complainte de mon obscurité deux," from *Vingt-cinq poèmes*, quoted in Tristan Tzara, *Oeuvres* (Seghers, 1952, rev. ed., 1960), p. 122. Compare Ernest Fenellosa ("An Essay on the Chinese Written Character," in Ezra Pound's *Instigations*, 1920, reprinted 1967 [Essay Index Reprint Series, Books for Libraries Press, Freeport, N.Y.], p. 386). The poet's metaphors, says Fenellosa, triumph over "the dead white plaster of copula" by a thousand shades of verbal coloration. "His figures flood things with jets of various light, like the sudden up-blaze of fountains." Like Benjamin Péret in his essays on Mayan language, like Owen Barfield in his *Poetic Diction: a Study in Meaning* (Faber and Gwyer, 1927; McGraw-Hill, 1964), Pound and Fenellosa stress the "primitive" attitude toward the concrete image as the starting point of genuine poetic diction, at the opposite pole from the abstractions of more "cultivated" language. A certain relationship can be seen with the Dadaist refusal of accepted (cultural) manifestations, to which they reply with their own, indisputably different.

[9] "Surface maladie," from *De nos oiseaux, ibid.*, p. 129.

que la vue ne s'accroche plus au-delà des montagnes
et des eaux. . .[10]

(the fountain escapes climbing
toward the other colors

in an ash-colored rainbow
the damp colors prowl about
intoxicated

dirtied dampened shred of night we have built
in each of us a tower of such lofty color
that our free gaze is caught no more beyond the
    mountains and the waters. . .)

At other times color is more closely identified with human sensitivity, either in a positive setting, where, for
instance, piano music runs multicolored through the listeners' brains like the metallic veins in rocks, or in a
negative one, where the aesthetic sense is violently as-
saulted. Here the colors become only numbers to be
liquidated, nervously circling in a setting more common
than universal:

les couleurs sont des chiffres qu'on tue et qui sautent
carrousel
comme tout le monde[11]

(the colors are numbers murdered and leaping
carousel
like everyone)

[10] "Règle," from "Indicateur des chemins de coeur," *MC*, p.
106.
[11] "Cinéma calendrier du coeur abstrait," *MC*, p. 31. "Tout le
monde" can also be read ironically, depending on whether one
finds the spectacle ordinary or not.

This vulgar circling of the carousel is preceded by the spontaneous belly-dance of a balloon, in opposition to the calm checkerboard of a landscape, just as a woman in kilometers of green rubber makes a startling contrast to the static and deadly white "cordes du minuit atrophié" in a later section of the same poem. In this poem and in many others the two obvious centers of Tzara's early poetry, color and motion, are joined in an association exactly represented by the circus image he so frequently uses.[12]

[12] For an interesting note on the importance of the circus for the futurist imagination, see Peter Wollen, *Signs and Meaning in the Cinema* (University of Indiana Press, 1969).

The relation of the futurist attitude to those discussed in these essays is worth considering at length: as capsule examples, however, we might take the following points in futurist theories (for the history and the products of futurism, see Marianne W. Martin, *op. cit.* and Joshua Taylor, *Futurism*, Museum of Modern Art, 1961). 1) The proclamations about the infinite and the open: for instance, the ABOLITION OF THE FINITE LINE AND CLOSED SCULPTURE (in Boccioni's *Technical Manifesto of Futurist Painting of 1910*), are not unlike the surrealist stress on the unknown in preference to the known, the open in preference to the limited, the refusal of the merely linear; whereas the bridge Boccioni demands between the EXTERIOR PLASTIC INFINITE and the INTERIOR PLASTIC INFINITE could be related to the notion of an interior model, the communicating vessels, and so on. 2) The search for "The Style of Movement" (from the Bernheim-Jeune catalogue for the Futurist exhibition in Paris, 1912) is clearly also the object of all these essays. Boccioni's declaration, "I want to fix the human form in movement" is, as it were, the underlying epigraph, including the will to fixity with that other will, not necessarily opposed, to motion. 3) The effort toward the "naked" purity of the noun and its "essential color" (Marinetti in *Les Mots en liberté futuristes*, ed. Futuriste di *Poesia*, 1919) is an effort continually urged in the Dada manifestos ("Flow in all colors. . . .") and notes on art. (Compare the latter and the quotations from them made here with the ideas of Gaetano Previati as Marianne Martin quotes him on p. 58: "Our pictorial

By the constant stress on color, movement, and contrast, the poet is sure of forcing the reader's attention,
his avowed aim: "We are circus managers." (*SMD*, p.
15) The ever-present consciousness of the poem as performance makes the choice of circus imagery doubly

---

sensations can no longer be whispered. We shall make them
sing and shout on our canvasses which will blare forth [with]
deafening and triumphant fanfares . . . beneath our skin brown
does not course, but . . . yellow sparkles, red blazes, and . . .
green, blue, and violet dance voluptuously and caressingly there.
. . . Your eyes accustomed to dimness will be opened to the most
radiant visions of light. The shadows which we shall paint will
be more luminous than the highlights of our predecessors; and
our pictures, compared to those stored in museums, will be as a
refulgent day to a gloomy night.") Compare also Carrà in his
Manifesto on *The Painting of Sounds, Noises, Odours* (*Lacerba*,
no. 17, Aug., 1913, quoted in Martin, p. 136): "THE PAINTING
OF SOUNDS, NOISES, AND ODOURS DENIES. . . . Greys, browns, . . .
the pure horizontal, the pure vertical. . . . The right angle. . . .
The *cube* . . . (and) WANTS . . . Reds, Reeeds that screeeeeeeam
. . . greeeeeens that shrieeeeeek . . . the dynamic arabesque. . . .
The sphere, the whirling ellipse . . . the spiral and all the dynamic forms which the . . . artist's genius can discover." Péret's
reds so bright they roll in continual motion, Tzara's poetry as it
shrieks along, gouging out craters in its path, are close relatives
of this statement. Compare also Tzara's praise of the *découpage
cinématographique* as a technique of multiplication, synthesis,
and dynamization, the "précipitation cinétique et rotative
d'images d'un monde accéléré," *Les Cahiers d'art*, no. 37, p.
195. Although Tzara abounds in eulogies for the techniques of
collage—of Apollinaire's *Calligrammes*, for example—and of
verbal superimpositions—in his preface to Tristan Corbière's
Amours jaunes (Le Club des Amis du Livre, 1950)—he is in
violent disagreement with the "academic" side of the cubists and
even the futurists, attacking the former for their static position,
the latter for their excessive use of traditional subject matter:

Le cubisme naquit de la simple façon de regarder l'objet:
Cézanne peignait une tasse 20 centimètres plus bas que ses
yeux, les cubistes la regardent d'en haut, d'autres compliquent
l'apparence en faisant une section perpendiculaire et en l'ar-

appropriate; even the belly-dance and the piano concert mentioned above can and probably should be considered self-referential, but the circus poems demonstrate such an attitude with the greatest clarity. Many of Tzara's poems start with a command, "regarde-moi." Others incorporate a testimony to the crucial role of vision: "voir," "vois mon visage," "regardez monsieur,"[13]

rangeant sagement à côté. . . . Le futuriste voit la même tasse en mouvement, succession d'objets l'un à côté de l'autre et ajoute malicieusement quelques lignes-forces. Cela n'empêche que la toile soit une bonne ou mauvaise peinture destinée au placement des capitaux intellectuels. (*SMD*, pp. 23-24)

In this passage Tzara seems to underestimate the Futurist innovations by associating them with subject matter more properly called cubist (the futurists do not, after all, *usually* concern themselves with the depiction of cups and saucers) for reasons which are not hard to fathom. For an interesting viewpoint on Tzara's work on Apollinaire, see Guillaume Apollinaire, *Les Peintres Cubistes* (présentation L. C. Breunig et J.-Cl. Chevalier, Hermann, coll. Miroirs de l'Art, 1965).

4) An immense line is said to join distant and "seemingly hostile things," like the *fil conducteur* of surrealism. Some of the various techniques of analogy—for example, that of following a substantive by its double—are familiar techniques of Dada and surrealist writing. Of course, surrealism places the accent on identity rather than on succession, whereas the evocation of "the moments of an object" is the goal of futurism; in this as in a number of other ways the attitudes are profoundly different. But strong likeness of techniques and of theory remains. All the notions of dynamism, simultaneity, *bruitisme*, *nunisme* (and even the mechanical whirling of vorticism, whose still center, however, places it closer to surrealism—"l'homme au centre du tourbillon"—than to futurism) should at least be compared with the poetic passion for circus. The kinship of attitude is as clear as the differences. (See also note 8 to the Cendrars chapter and note 11 to the Péret chapter.)

[13] A good example of the visible and circular linking of some of this poetry (the word "progression" is perhaps too strong) is "Le Dompteur de lions se souvient," which begins with the specific "regardez-moi" and ends with the general "voir."

as an active invocation of the reader's glance as well
as a reminder from the poet to himself of the essential
showmanship expected in his poetry. The Dada cata-
logues of spectacle are spectacularly self-conscious col-
lages formed of bits of sounds, partial sights, cacopho-
nies of shouting colors in motion, and more particularly,
of signals to the reader about the reading of the poem,

STOP[14]
(STOP)

ATTENTION c'est la plaie que je sonde[15]
(WATCH OUT it's the wound I'm probing)

(applaudir ici)[16]
(applaud here)

ICI LA COULEUR[17]
(COLOR HERE),

its purpose ("je dis cela pour t'amuser"[18]), or its probable effect ("ma chère si tu as mal à cause des sons tu
dois prendre une pillule"[19]). Having already accepted
the telegraphic form, the reader is not bothered by differences of level or pitch among the elements of the
collage; the poem is visible simultaneously as are all the
rings of the circus.

Each of the *Vingt-cinq poèmes* shrieks at the reader
and engages him in its own dizziness and internal multiplication of motion:

[14] "Arc," *De nos oiseaux.* [15] "Boxe I," *ibid.*
[16] "Boxe II," *ibid.* [17] "Boxe III," *ibid.*
[18] "Réalités cosmiques vanille tabac éveils," *ibid.*
[19] "Sainte," *Vingt-cinq poèmes* (Collection Dada, 1918).

ici intervient le tambour major et la cliquette
car il y a des zigzags sur son âme et beaucoup de
    r r r r r r r ici le lecteur commence à crier
il commence à crier commence à crier puis dans
    ce cri il y a des flutes qui se multiplient des corails[20]
écoute écoute écoute j'avale mbampou et ta bonne
    volonté
prends danse entends viens tourne bois vire ouhou
    ouhou ouhou (mouvement)[21]

(here the drum-major breaks in and the castanets
for there are zigzags on his soul and many r r r r r r r's
    here the reader starts shouting
he starts shouting shouting and then in this shout
    there are flutes proliferating corals
listen listen listen I am swallowing mbampou and
    your good will
take dance listen come turn drink swerve ouhou
    ouhou ouhou [motion])

There is no space provided within the poem for the briefest lapse of attention; neither the volume nor the intensity can be diminished in this poetry intended as a

concentration intérieure craquement des mots qui
crèvent crépitent les décharges électriques[22]

(inner concentration cracking of words
collapsing crackling electric volleys)

Dada poetry is meant to elicit not the educated responses of cultured sensitivity, but rather the instant

[20] "Le géant blanc lépreux du paysage," *ibid.*
[21] "Mouvement," *ibid.*   [22] "Sainte," *ibid.*

and incoherent primitive reactions of the eye and ear. If it permits no slow-moving intellectual translations, it seems to carry its own rapid and external indications of a possible (or, as Tzara would say, necessary) interior ordering. But since we cannot directly glimpse the internal order, our changing views of the poem are likely to remain disordered, fragmented, and bewildering. The structural or thematic links we perceive on the surface *may* or *may not* lie parallel to the unheard rhythm within: the ambiguity is essential to the Dada spirit. We can either place our faith in Tzara's guarantee of an intuitive luminous architecture or accept his only half-humorous assurance that Dada's obscurity is so dark as eventually to create its own light; then again, we may, perhaps most wisely, follow his insistent advice that we look at the Dada poem as a simple spectacle, at the Dada gesture as a creation complete in itself and completely indescribable. "Art is at present the only construction entire in itself, of which nothing further can be said, it is so completely richness, vitality, sense, wisdom. To understand, to see. Describe a flower: relative poetry more or less paper flower. See." (*SMD*, p. 85)

3. BEYOND THE CIRCUS

After 1924, Tzara's references to language are gradually embodied in a less self-conscious imagery, as if his reflection on the rôle the word might play could finally be separated from the specific words of the poem itself. Parallel with that development, the potential power of language as Tzara conceives it spreads out to the world beyond the human circus, as some of the surprisingly

71

static and aging images of Dada (where, for example, a white tongue is pictured as part of a rotting crystal, where language is seen as transparent but transfixed— "la chanson cristallisée/ dans le/ vase du corps"[23] the song crystallized / in the / vase of the body) take on the far more active quality shown by the image of the "cristaux chanteurs."[24] From the song crystallized in a passive form to the crystal itself singing, the distance is great.

Two qualities remain constant in Tzara's repeated imagery of the word: while the possible obscurity of language or thought is compared to figures of cold, to snow crazed, absurd, or awkward ("les neiges lourdes"),[25] to an icy spectre as a guide to a false path, language in its clearest form (including the decidedly garish clarity of Dada colors) is compared to heat and to light, as the simplest source of vision:

La parole seule suffit pour voir[26]

(The word alone suffices for seeing)

Now the edges of words burn their surroundings, cutting a luminous path for human desire. In three successive poems from *A Perte de nuages* of 1930, Tzara identifies shadow with the negation of language, sometimes a more satisfying state than its presence: ("douce absence de mots où l'ombre vient s'embrouiller"[27] / sweet

---

[23] "Verre traverser paisible," *ibid.*
[24] "Date," *L'Arbre des voyageurs* (ed. de la Montagne, 1930).
[25] *Loc. cit.*
[26] *L'Homme approximatif* (Gallimard, coll. Poésie, 1968), p. 33.
[27] "Rappel," in *L'Arbre des voyageurs.*

absence of words where the shadow intersperses) or with its distance from us, as if that distance sufficed to put the verbal gesture into mourning ("les sombres mots de lointain"[28] / the somber far-off words) while the fiery touch of language is identified with vitality, height, and presence:

chantantes fièvres aériennes

. . .

fondant en feu hurleur tout l'avenir[29]

(singing airy fevers

. . .

melting in a raging fire all the future)

But even here in the presence of language, deception eventually sets in, as the perhaps inevitable double of Dada/surrealist hope; here the fire of words can no longer reach the source: "le feu de paroles n'atteint plus le brasier."[30] In 1935, the imagery of cold and darkness gradually permeates the world of the word. In spite of the optimistic charge of the verb "pressentie" in the following quotation from *La Main passe*, in spite of all the suggestions of intimacy, a strong note of despair is evident:

les seins de la parole pressentie
à l'orée de la neige
la chaîne noire du chant
. . .

[28] "Date," *ibid.* [29] *Loc. cit.*
[30] "Le Dégel des ombres," *ibid.*

73

> qu'importent mes phrases et la chaleur dont je
> voudrais les entourer[31]

> (the breasts of the word sensed
> at the rim of the snow
> the black chain of the song
>
> . . .
>
> what do my phrases matter and the warmth with
> which I would like to surround them)

Soon the cold has spread to the once vital center of action. In *Les Mutations radieuses* (1935-36) the word is noble but fated, it is harsh, even statuesque in profile but nevertheless ephemeral, fated to pass with the passing seasons:

> et vous paroles de marbre heures éternelles plutôt
> périssables
> que dures plutôt rudes voyelles des temps
> saisonniers[32]

> (and you marble words eternal hours more
> perishable
> than lasting harsher vowels of seasonable weather)

On a page of an early manuscript, set apart in a box to signal its importance, is the optimistic slogan: *Les Mots de passe*, the passwords. But toward the end of his life, Tzara used for a group of writings a title which can be read as the opposite signal: *Les Mots de paille*,[33] the words of straw. From the idea of language as the passport to a spectacular and brilliantly active (if illu-

---

[31] "Les Forêts de la mémoire," in *Midis gagnés* (Denöel, 1939).
[32] "Le Géant des murs," *ibid.*
[33] In *Parler seul* (Maeght, 1950; Caractères, 1955).

sory) universe to that of a language more modest in scope and in composition, the change in vision is marked. It appears, even more significantly, a change as to the place and the tone of action. The season of the circus seems to have gone forever, and with it the time of manifesto and spectacular.

Tzara chose from the beginning to make language synonymous with action, to equate the force of words with speed of movement: we cannot choose to have it otherwise. As the interior dynamism of words is sapped, they lose their formerly *theatrical* momentum. This interpretation may seem unwontedly tragic, undeservedly cynical as to the possible joining of poetry and practical action, and yet from the point of view taken here, from *inside* the theatre of poetry, there is no bridge to outside judgment. The profile of the gesture can be sketched without an estimate as to its efficacy, the particular tone of poetic language described apart from the details it may narrate, the specific intensity of the brushstroke evaluated with no reference to the object depicted. In this case it is not a matter of arbitrarily choosing a formalistic approach, but of taking Tzara's own counsel about the necessary poetic stance before the *gesture* of art: "See."

C. *Benjamin Péret's Game and Gesture*

> Et emporté par le courant
> j'ai traversé des contrées sans
> lumière et sans voix
>
> (*Le Grand jeu*)

et je danserai devant ces
    fameuses pyramides
jusqu'à ce qu'elles disparaissent.

(*Immortelle maladie*)

This final chapter in the poetry of rapid and visible motion is devoted to Benjamin Péret, a poet of spectacular gesture and uncompromising (surrealist) attitude. To use an optimistic title conferred on a reprinting of one of his essays by his friends and admirers, *La Parole est à Péret:*[1] it is Péret's turn to be heard.

1. A LANGUAGE OF EXPLOSION

Faithful to the surrealist movement until his death, Péret has often been considered the most remarkable poet of that movement, its ideal spokesman of spontaneity. He is known for his unrelenting defense of human liberty against what he calls its clerical and capitalist oppressors, his constant testimonies to the idea of an *amour sublime,* and especially for the easy brilliance of his poetic imagery. The most direct of all the surrealist poets, he casually displays the effortless, perfect language of abundance and explosion that was demanded also of the Dada poet. Péret's work has not often been given the kind of recognition it deserves, except by the surrealists themselves, and by the "surréalisants." As a person, he has been admired for his intransigence, for his colorful personality and habits, while his writings have been admired for reasons of the same order—that is, for their colorful images and for

[1] New York, Editions Surréalistes, 1943. (Hereafter referred to as *PP.*)

their irreverence. But beyond those characteristics shared by a number of surrealist writers, his poetry often shows a more *consistent* intensity than other surrealist poems, and a more determinedly explosive nature: lyricism is here subordinated to rapidity of metamorphosis, and yet heightened by it.

Péret's own definition of his poetry surpasses any we could give: "J'appelle tabac ce qui est oreille." (I call by the name tobacco what is really an ear.)[2] The statement compresses four possible elements into three, eliminating the middle term and strengthening the newly forged link between the others. The suppressed term "mouth" is the underlying link between "calling" or naming verbally and hearing or understanding (*entendre* in both senses, a verb suppressed but present by implication); the mouth is also the obvious location for the tobacco's consumption.

J'appelle tabac ce qui est oreille

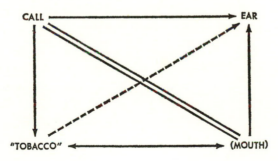

[2] "Qui est-ce," *Benjamin Péret* (ed. *Poètes d'aujourd'hui*, Seghers, 1961), p. 96. (Hereafter referred to as *PA*.) The possible link between "appeler" and "oreille," that is, between language and listening, was suggested to me by Sarah Lawall.

All the while the statement points to its own unusual procedure (if it were not to be considered out of the ordinary, why would he ask for our attention to it: "I call"?)

Poetic language in its deliberate shiftings of perception and appellation is akin to magic and to madness. It is further identified with revolution. Against the "mummified words" of priests and their "paralysing gods,"[3] Péret demands a language always sacrilegious and a spirit of permanent blasphemy. Heretics question the bases of myth and thus prevent the collective exaltation of a people from hardening into dogma, whereas priests are, according to Péret, the assassins of poetry. He admires Breton for recognizing in the concept of surrealist love the "explosive center of human life,"[4] while he himself attributes to it a power of vertiginous luminosity. The ambiguous motion this sort of understanding provokes and its equally ambiguous stillness ("the point of departure and arrival of all desire") are at least as important for him as the illumination. While Breton emphasizes the crystalline images—those of fire, sparks, salt cubes, glass chains—Péret speaks mostly of symmetrical motion, colorful rather than crystalline, of the vertical ascension toward a love he calls "sublime," of the geometrical *place* of love and of poetry,[5] the two elements not to be separated one from the other.

[3] In *Minotaure*, no. 11.

[4] *Anthologie de l'amour sublime* (Albin Michel, 1956), p. 67. (Hereafter referred to as *AS*.)

[5] Péret sees his "amour sublime" as the reachable summit of desire, in lofty contrast both with the "bassesse" of the social con-

Three of Péret's poems, spanning a thirty-year period, can be taken as reliable descriptions of the road leading to the summit of surrealist poetry. "Le Mariage des feuilles," in *Le Grand Jeu* of 1928 begins with the discovery of a "circular poetry," which rolls and sways until the final perception where the ordinarily majestic is deliberately softened to accommodate the swervings of poetic rhythm:

des grandes montagnes molles
où tournent virent et plongent
les chaussons de danse (*GJ*, 103)

(great soft mountains
where dancing-slippers
spin circle and swoop)

---

dition and with the "grossièreté" of purely sensual love. Breton's implicit contrast of "l'amour fou" and reasonable love considers two things to be imagined on the same plane if at opposite poles, whereas "l'amour sublime" is a deliberate use of *vertical* imagery. Péret's fascination with the hard geometrical precision of the diamond and of the "point-limite" is a strong reminder of Breton's "point sublime" and his "éloge du cristal," but Péret carries the geometrical sharpness even further than Breton. It has often been remarked that all Breton's work shows a transformational process—in his picture of dream and reality as two "vases communicants" he presents a kind of fluidity and interchange which the perfect crystalline structure he speaks of does not have. Péret never gives any place to this sort of flexible compromise: for him, even poetry is a "lieu géométrique" and only a being with the poetic spark can possibly aspire to the other geometric place which is "l'amour sublime." Rigidity of spirit, asceticism and sacrifice are the basis for the harsh purity of this perfect love, in which the lovers exalt each other in an always symmetrical movement, "jusqu'à constituer un complexe à la fois religieux et magique" (*AS*, p. 53).

79

Contrast and shock, such as those produced by the notion of softened mountains,[6] are of course the necessary
ingredients of a poetry representing the revolutionary
imagination.

In "Toute une vie" of 1949, Péret compares Breton's
launching of the first *Manifesto* to a bomb thrown in the
courtyard, its energy and force the obvious opposites
of a pathetic old man, who is only capable of sighing
faintly and readjusting his mashed-potato gaze. The
poet has no sympathy for nonforceful beings, whose
lack of imagination condemns them as surely as would
any sin. The old poetry, this *past* poetry of which they
are the partisans and the creators, an immobile relic
stuffed like a captured or domestic animal, has come
apart at the seams, and yet the insects which have
(properly) reduced it to its present state of useless
trophy are joined in a fitting poetic juxtaposition to the
agents of liberation:

Les hirondelles des mots qui ouvrent les persiennes
du matin
s'envolaient à tire-d'ailes
franchissant les déserts de squelettes polis par les
vautours (*PA*, 131)

(The swallows of words opening the shutters of
morning
flew off swiftly
crossing the deserts of skeletons polished by
vultures)

[6] Compare the images of softened bookshelves and ripened
rocks in Breton's early poems.

In this atmosphere of nonfertility and nonrejuvenation, the vultures have picked over the bones of all the previous incarnations of poetry as thoroughly as the mites have feasted on the insides of the very newest old poetry. And yet the swallows return every season "plus agiles qu'un cri et sûres d'annoncer la naissance des eaux claires" (more agile than a cry and certain to announce the birth of clear waters), with a new strength of language and a new certainty of future births and brightness.

In the sections directly following, Péret envisions the dream set loose from the cell, where Christ-faced spiders had imprisoned its revolutionary gestures. Again, the poet perceives youthful expression and the potentiality of language as they are paralyzed by a static condition which implies a certain passing of time, so that the spiders are in some way parallel to the mites and the vultures, to the parasites of an outmoded culture, the harbingers of age and death. The liberated dream runs madly through a house, before rushing in a torrent down the steps in order to carry the surrealist revolution to the street, its only weapon being the energy of its spirit, its "regard à arracher les serrures" in direct opposition to the old man's mushy stare, his "regard de purée." And now the voice of the revolution confers on Péret's listener, who has been used only to the stubborn declamations of age, to hypocrisy and to mental imprisonment, an extreme clarity and the baptism of dawn and dew:

Pour me donner l'heure des baignades de lucidité
dans des eaux d'éclair

Et des lueurs d'aube teintaient de rosée leur visage
  de mineurs
Liberté liberté couleur d'homme
avais-tu déjà crié au milieu d'oreilles en ciment
  armé (*PA*, 132)

(To confer on me the moment of clear bathing in
  sparkling waters
And glimmers of dawn gave a dewy tint to their
  miners' faces
Freedom freedom color of man
you had already shouted amid ears of reinforced
  concrete)

All the gods and statues of former reverence have
turned to a dust of texts that would hide, if it were possible, the awakening of future liberty and darken the
transparency of the clear waters just reborn ("la fontaine aux ailes de vent du matin"/ the fountain winged
with morning wind [*PA*, 132]), that image associated
in a correspondence of clarity and fluidity with the
morning dew. The action of the wind and the water is
expansive or liberating in the same way as surrealist
language and love are, while the fragments of "textes"
resemble the past literature which was not, in whatever
form it was couched, poetry. A new gesture requires a
new language sufficiently strong to release the certain
bonds of the past, clearing a luminous space for all the
possible mirages of the future.

Language is seen as the imparter of consciousness;
when Péret says that in Breton a poetic consciousness
explodes "de tous ses oiseaux" (with all its birds) he is

paying him the highest compliment a surrealist can offer or accept, that of creating a convulsively free beauty which has nothing whatsoever in common with the stuffed parakeet to be trodden on, and everything in common with the swallows who fly off in the morning light.

The title of one of Péret's last poems, "Des cris étouffés"/ "Stifled cries" (1957), would appear a decided contrast to a language which explodes. It is certainly a quieter poem, written in the repetitious and yet progressive form we may call the surrealist litany, *if* we are careful to strip from that term any nuance of religious memory still clinging to it (see Péret's own attack on Eluard as a writer of civic litanies, in *Le Déshonneur des poètes*).[7] Beginning with a statement of faith in dialogue—listening and response being among the most serious forces of Péret's universe—this remarkable poem centers on a description of painful poetic sensitivity, and of the contrasting but parallel expressions of happiness and human response to the outside world:

Celui qui souffre d'une blessure en croissant de lune
   au front du jour
Celui qui gémit du passage à reculons du bleu de
   ciel entre des racines de cathédrales sans dieu
Celui qui entend

. . .

Celui qui rit comme un pré fleuri tandis que les
   martins-pêcheurs montent une garde en explosions

[7] *Le Déshonneur des poètes* (Mexico City, Poésie et Révolution, 1945). That this particular poem should be written in the

Celui qui répond par je t'aime au chant ensoleillé
des ailes froissant la verdure qui tête
Celui qui dit je t'aime à la première nacre du
soleil . . .
Celui qui du plein midi sut extraire le bruissement
inconnu des soudaines métamorphoses. . .

(*PA*, 135-36)

(He who suffers from a wound like the moon's
crescent on the forehead of day
He who moans at the receding passage of sky blue
between the roots of godless cathedrals
He who hears

. . .

He who laughs like a flowering meadow while
kingfishers keep explosive watch
He who answers I love you to the sunlit song of
wings ruffling the suckling grass
He who says I love you to the dawn's mother of
pearl . . .
He who knows how to extract from high noon the
unknown rustling of sudden metamorphoses. . .)

Here the image of the god fallen in the dust is repeated,
but the poet's action is entirely positive, as he moves
at a gallop toward the conquest of the gods themselves
behind the dust. The poet not only conquers for himself, but he also asserts a victory over the dust for those
not able to be conquerors, in a universal heroic gesture.
Going beyond the deserts with the wind, he transports

"litanic" form is especially interesting in view of these "cathédrales sans dieu"; the structure remains.

with him the earliest and most primitive signs of eternal sunlight (given forth by "des soleils sans fin"/ endless suns) his language a limitless language of high noon, of explosion and metamorphosis. The poet is at once the one who calls, the one who listens, and the one who answers: the multiplicity of the poem is the essential ground of the inclusive and expansive gesture of the greatest surrealist poetry.

2. THE GEOMETRICAL PLACE

One of the most striking situations for the privileged encounter of surrealist love and liberated language is the repetitive or litanic form already mentioned. Peculiarly appropriate to the notion of a geometrical place, it provides a definite structure against which the poetic gesture can be clearly observed. Here the contrast between exterior or obvious outline and the interior shiftings and transpositions of mood and images is strongly marked, and the poetry reveals an inner movement on a completely different level from that ordinarily associated with surrealist juxtapositions of imagery.

In the collection *Je sublime* (1936) there are two poems whose throwaway titles, "Allo" and "Clin d'oeil," mock their inner complexity. The first does not resemble a love poem until the end, when all the apparently heterogeneous images are seen in retrospect as defining in quite subtle ways the feeling of the poet for the woman loved:

Mon avion en flammes mon château inondé de vin du Rhin

mon ghetto d'iris noir mon oreille de cristal. . .
mon revolver de corail dont la bouche m'attire
 comme l'oeil d'un puits
scintillant glacé comme le miroir où tu contemples
 la fuite des oiseaux-mouches de ton regard
perdu dans une exposition de blanc encadrée de
 momies
je t'aime (*PA,* 106)

(My airplane in flames my castle flooded with
 Rhenish wine
My black iris ghetto my crystal ear. . .
my coral revolver's mouth drawing me like the eye
 of a glistening well
icy as the mirror where you observe the flight
 of the hummingbirds of your look
lost in a linen show framed with mummies
I love you)

Here the images do not serve as adjectives to describe her; she is, rather, all these things. The initial choppiness leads to the final long complex image with its shifting perspectives and to the simple concluding revelation, which might have been banal at the poem's beginning but is not at its end. Here all the lesser preliminary images develop into a rapid crescendo and are then subsumed under the extreme terseness of the final statement, "Rosa," its brevity reinforcing its importance. The cascading images lead to a reality whose further elaboration is unnecessary, whose simplicity is the more remarkable for the profusion that has preceded it. Within the poem itself, there is an interior cohesion of images:

the abundance of wine is later echoed by an "inondation de cassis"; a black foam of hair is followed by a rain of red grasshoppers; and a hidden pond, by a sparkling well iced over. The world seems very full, although it consists in reality of only one being; it contains snails, mosquitoes, birds of paradise, gazelles and butterflies, opals and turquoise, grapes and onions, all in twenty lines. Péret's personal exuberance is transformed directly into the enthusiastic gesture of his poetry. The coincidence of this expansive enthusiasm with simplicity is perhaps the salient characteristic of Péret's best poems.

Unlike "Allo," "Clin d'oeil" situates itself immediately as a straightforward love poem:

> Des vols de perroquets traversent ma tête quand je
>   te vois de profil
> et le ciel de graisse se strie d'éclairs bleus
> qui tracent ton nom dans tous les sens (*PA*, 107)

> (Flights of parakeets speed by my head when I
>   see your profile
> and the greasy sky is streaked with blue glimmers
> tracing out your name in all directions)

The blue-green color of the parakeets leads directly to the spectacle of the blue flashes in the sky, reflecting the emotional vision which dominates in its clarity the sullen and unpleasant natural background. But the poem moves quickly beyond mere spectacle toward a singular intersubjectivity, where gestures are shared and thus intensified:

> où les seins aigus des femmes regardent par les yeux
>   des hommes

87

Aujourd'hui je regarde par tes cheveux
Rosa d'opale du matin
et je m'éveille par tes yeux
Rosa d'armure
et je pense par tes seins d'explosion (*PA*, 107)

(where the pointed breasts of women stare out
    through the eyes of men
Today I look out through your hair
Rosa of morning opal
and I wake up through your eyes
Rosa of armor
and I think through your exploding breasts)

Surrealism wages war on the principle of personal identity and values love and game precisely for their destruction of egoism, as *L'Amour fou* and *L'Amour sublime* are the successors of the sublime game of *Le Grand jeu* (or "Le Grand je") and the *Je sublime* (or the "Jeu sublime," or even, in so far as surrealist poetry is always an elevation, a transformation and transmutation "for the better," an act of making *sublime*, as the verb form "I make sublime" is the most appropriate one for this particular poetic action, this poetic game). Finally game and poetic act are absorbed in the all-inclusive language of juncture, one which permits no separations.

The end of the poem is deceptively simple, as the last line assumes within itself all the accumulated qualities of the other lines, the profusion of messages ("timbres-poste"), the images of lightness ("fumée de cigares" and "écume de mer"), and those of the final synthesis in clarity; here the crystal repeats the mirror and the crystal ear of the preceding poem:

Rosa de forêt noire inondée de timbres-poste bleus
et verts
Rosa de fumée de cigare
Rosa d'écume de mer faite cristal
Rosa (*PA*, 107)

(Rosa of black forest drenched with blue-green
postage stamps
Rosa of cigar smoke
Rosa of sea foam made crystal
Rosa)[8]

As in Péret's poem of liquid imagery discussed above, the images reflect each other; the greens and blues of the stamps are the colors of the parakeets, and the smoke and foam are changed into the clarity of the crystal as the *blue* flashes of the name *Rosa*[9] make bright streaks in the greasy sky. Unlike the woman described by a normal linguistic pattern in Breton's famous poem "L'Union libre" ("Ma femme aux yeux de savane . . ."), Rosa is not described as *having* shoulders of champagne: she is *of* morning opal, etc. Breton's catalogue of attributes is very different from Péret's perception of *coalescence*. It is as if there were a certain comfortable distance, a breathing space, among the elements of

[8] *Le Grand jeu* (Gallimard, 1928, coll. Poésie, 1969). (Hereafter referred to as *GJ*.)

[9] Compare the transformations of ordinary images, colors, and materials in André Breton, *Premier manifeste* (*Manifestes du surréalisme*, Pauvert, 1963, p. 63): "Cet été *les roses sont bleues*; le bois c'est du verre" (italics mine).

Breton's universe, between the poet and the woman, the woman and her qualities. Péret's poetry leaves none, since the poet himself wakes up through her eyes, and since she is literally part of that which in most poems she would only resemble.

In a poem of 1942, "Où es-tu," the complexity appears not in the woman but in the poet loving her.

> Je voudrais te parler cristal fêlé hurlant comme
>   un chien dans une nuit de draps battants
> comme un bateau démâté que la mousse de la mer
>   commence d'envahir
> où le chat minaule parce que tous les rats sont
>   partis[10]

> (I should like to speak to you cracked crystal
>   howling like a dog in a night of flapping sheets
> like an unmasted ship just invaded by sea foam
> where the cat miauls at the rats' departure)

Here the initial ambiguity lies in the "cristal fêlé"—to whom does it apply, the person addressed or the poet? Since Péret so often thinks of Baudelaire, we may remember "La Cloche fêlée" and assume that the poet feels himself in some way damaged. The rest of the poem bears out this supposition; "Je voudrais te parler comme . . ." introduces two more sets of catastrophic descriptions. After the howling and the sinking, there is a tree overturned in a storm, a series of ripped-out telephone wires, the noise of a door being broken down, a subway train stalled, a toe with a splinter sticking in

[10] From *Un Point c'est tout*, in Benjamin Péret, *Oeuvres complètes, II* (Le Terrain vague, 1971), p. 193.

90

it, a sterile vine, a cold hearth, a deserted café. The form becomes more and more intricate until there are seven clauses depending one on the other, linked less awkwardly than one would expect by a line of utterly banal words: "Avec . . . dans . . . pareil à . . . dans . . . qui . . . que . . . où . . . comme . . . dans . . . qui . . . que . . . où. . . ." But the surface is totally smooth and leads to a deceptively quiet conclusion after all the images of negation and violence, an end no less ambiguous than the beginning:

Je te dirais simplement
que je t'aime comme le grain de blé aime le soleil
se levant en haut de sa tête de merle

(I should simply say to you
that I love you as the grain of wheat loves the sun
rising above its blackbird head)

Is the sudden transposition to the humility of the natural world (the modesty of "le grain de blé") a deliberate rejection of the language ordinarily available to the poet? In any case, the golden wheat identified with the dark bird hovering just above it provides the clash of colors, a junction of visual opposites which plays against the simultaneous vertical attraction by resemblance, just as the brevity, simplicity, and uncertainty of the first line contrast with the repeated assurance, the length, and the tripartite metaphor of the second.

Here tragic effect depends on detail. The conditional form, "Je te dirais," holds out no hope of being able to speak the love in reality, while the question "Où es-tu" of the title implies the absence even of the person spoken to, if speech were possible. In spite of its formal and visual effect, the poem remains then, inevitably, in the realm of the merely possible. Perhaps that is the most fitting *place* for such poetry, the underlying justification for its unique status. Ironically, the poem comes from a group called *Un point c'est tout*. Like so many of Péret's titles, it cuts away the ground from under all interpretations and places a definitive end right at the beginning, a process as unreasonable and as intelligent as surrealism itself.

3. PROTRUSION AND EXTENSION

But even beyond the privileged place of the litany, the gestures typical of Péret are not those used by the other surrealists. In most of his poems, a movement of rapid transposition, augmentation, illogical extension, or a sudden stopping of movement gives its character to the text. Since these motions are often seemingly unrelated to the rest of the poem, they protrude sharply from the textual space into our own, forcing our attention in a way that poems all of one piece may not. When we have become sensitive to this sort of explosion outward from the text, other less immediately visible gestures apparently incorporated into the flow of the poem stand out within the text itself. The following characteristic examples, ranging from blatant to subtle, are grouped by the *kinds* of movement they represent.

In a technique appropriate to Péret's statement already used to define his notion of poetry ("J'appelle tabac ce qui est oreille"), the motion of a gesture may be reversed from its ordinary direction. Thus, in a poem called "Nue nue comme ma maîtresse," what is re-flected is that which ordinarily reflects:

à cause de vous dont la nudité reflète des miroirs
(because of you whose nakedness reflects mirrors)

The fact that Péret is addressing a "belle de bouteille" has probably been forgotten when this image appears; even if it is remembered, there is a slight (and purpose-ful) deformation of the traditional homage to one's mistress.

Or the gesture may be abbreviated deliberately. In a more serious vein (although couched in the tone of playfulness Péret frequently adopts), his *Histoire natu-relle* of 1945 offers the image of the freshly watered earth producing a "lipstick from which the kiss can be extracted" (*PA*, 174). The image can be read in two directions, either from the mark left by the activity then inferred from it, or from the color as a potential prepa-ration for the activity. In either case, the essential link omitted between the cosmetic and the activity com-presses the space of the image, thus forcing the accelera-tion of the rhythm.

The opposite process, by which the space is extended, and the gesture lengthened, is far more frequent. Péret refines a number of techniques of positive and negative extension, from the simplest verbal level ("etc. et mille fois etc.," *GJ*, 147) or typographical peculiarities ("Le caniche grossit grossit grossit grossit" *GJ*, 182) to the level of image,

et je vous attends au bord de la figure vii
où les anneaux de mes yeux s'enchaînent comme
  des fleurs
où le bruit de mes pas croît comme une catapulte
  (*GJ*, 27)

(and I await you at the edge of the figure vii
where the rings of my eyes are linked like a flower
  chain
where the noise of my steps grows like a catapult)

to the rhythmic level, where the gradually increasing
tempo takes precedence over what would ordinarily be
considered the "sense" of the poem. "Sais-tu" (a half-
pun on the name of the collection in which it is found,
Un Point c'est tout), ends on a series of negative images,
any one of which would have sufficed to convey the
pessimistic intent. The momentum of the verbal gesture carries it along past the purely logical stopping-
place toward a lengthened and all the more pathetic
ending, combining a quiet personal desolation with the
natural and with the extraordinary:

où tu n'apparais pas plus qu'une feuille de nénuphar
  au fond des bois
pas plus qu'une fraise des bois dans une chambre
  à air
pas plus que ma vie au tournant de la rue (*PA*, 118)

(where you appear no more than a waterlily leaf in
  the forest depth
no more than a wild strawberry in an air chamber
no more than my life at the turning of the street)

A more complex example appears in a poem whose title even is as much exaggeration as it is cliché, "Mille fois," where an entire set of possible images is unfolded or extended from three conditions contrary to fact. ("If larks stood in line to be roasted, if water did not mix with wine, if I had five francs. . . .") After a series in brief catalogue form, a final longer image representing the qualities of lightness and unreality is spun out until the falsity of the condition is implicitly recognized and all ties to the world outside the poem are cut off in a sudden melancholy awareness:

il y aurait dans le creux de ma main
un petit lampion froid
doré comme un oeuf sur le plat
et si léger que la semelle de mes chaussures
    s'envolerait comme un faux nez
en sorte que le fond de la mer serait une cabine
    téléphonique
d'où personne n'obtiendrait jamais aucune
    communication (*PA*, 90)

(there would be in the hollow of my hand
a small cold lantern
gilded like a fried egg
and so light that the soles of my shoes would fly
    away like a false nose
so that the sea bottom would be a telephone booth
where no one could ever receive a call)

A study of the conclusions of Péret's poems provides the most revealing perspective on their framework and gesture. The motion of a poem extends often into the space beyond the actual text, sometimes negatively, by a self-conscious reference to its own limitation, or by the signs of its own incomplete nature, or both. A poem may end suddenly just as a reason is about to be given, so that the last word marks a logical beginning: "because." Or it may appeal to the reader's interest only to mock that interest immediately afterwards:

L'automobile serait sensationnelle[11]
huit roues deux moteurs
et au milieu un bananier
qui masquerait Adam et Eve
faisant
mais ceci fera l'objet d'un autre poème (*GJ*, 130)

(The automobile would be sensational
eight wheels two motors
and in the middle a banana shrub
hiding Adam and Eve
making
but that will be the subject of another poem)

[11] Péret's enthusiasm for the automobile and for all the other means of motion (see, a little farther on, the epic poem whose leit-motif runs: "Je partirai Sept lieues d'un coup de pédale") might be compared with the futurist admiration for the machine: for example, Marinetti's early poem to the racing automobile, which he calls his Pegasus:

> Dieu véhément d'une race d'acier,
> Automobile ivre d'espace
>
> . . .
> Je lâche enfin tes brides métalliques et tu t'élances,
> avec ivresse, dans l'infini libérateur. . . .

(quoted Martin, *op. cit.*) where the works of Mario Morasso in praise of the mechanized and the rapid ("The Aesthetics of Speed," "The Heroes of the Machine," "The Great Flight") are briefly discussed.

Here again the reverse technique is used, whereby the text closes itself off as unimportant, and the gesture deprecates its own movement with a line such as "Besides I don't see why we are talking about that"—while the absence of a period at the end indicates that the poet will not even attribute to the text its distinction as a separate text.

The *conclusion* of the gesture is spotlighted here, as the beginning seems often to be in the work of a more metaphysical poet such as Bonnefoy. Perhaps that appearance is due to the contrast between poems of rapid exterior motion, visible instantly—such as those of Péret—and those where the paradoxical image of a motionless path—Bonnefoy's "we moved in the immobile"—leads to an inner gesture.

4. EPIC

Apart from some of Aragon's early poems in *Feu de joie*, and a few texts of Breton (not those longer poems he might have called epic), apart from Tzara's *Homme approximatif*, there are not many surrealist poems of a consistently epic nature. The word is taken here in the sense of *epic gesture*, or epic theme, irrespective of the formal length, the larger-than-life hero, or the obvious intention. Three of Péret's poems in *Le Grand jeu* show different possible perspectives on that gesture: the heroic-tragic, the mock-heroic, and the irrational-marvelous.

"Samson" begins, in a semi-biblical tone, with the motifs of election, voyage, and chance: "Or nous délégués par les sceptres/ traversions les plaines lustrées par l'arachnéenne chance" (Now we appointed by sceptres/ were crossing the plains glazed by the spiderwebs of fate) (*GJ*, 33) and with a strong consciousness of personal power and a style appropriate to it. "Arrivez sources de ma main et réchauffez les ossements des glaciers" (Oh fountains of my hand arrive and warm the bones of glaciers). (*GJ*, 33) Then follows a warning, probably addressed only to nonheroes, that a somber or discouraged gaze may lead only to the making of curtseys (a *precious* contrast to the heroic voyage or, at the very least, located on a different scale). The hero himself may meet with danger, for the hills now seated on the "dead weight of lakes," with their feet "weeping" into the water, are soon destined to go forth on a road of blood leading them to rocks of torture. Nor is the road clearly marked—it begins to resemble a labyrinth, as the hill becomes the sign leading to the landscape, and the landscape becomes only the sign directing toward itself ("le pôteau de lui-meme"). The ancient gesture of traditional epic, regretted, can perhaps be recreated. Péret transforms, but not unrecognizably, the courtly themes of love, the lance, and the ship:

> et que l'orée soit l'étincelle qui va du cou de
>   l'amante à celui de l'amant
> et que se perde la lance dans la cervelle du temps
> et que la vague porte la poutre (*GJ*, 34)

> (and let the boundary be the spark that jumps
>   from the beloved's neck to that of her lover

and let the lance be lost in the brain of time
and let the wave bear the beam)

But the setting is not propitious. The poem ends slowly
on three sets of triple structures, the conclusion of each
being a tragic one: "Mais l'hirondelle ne sera jamais le
paysage. . . . Mais que le paysage découvre. . . . Mais
jamais les étoiles ne suivront le sillage des poissons
étoilés." After this denial of possibility (the whole cannot be made from the part: as in "one swallow does not
make a summer"—here the bird cannot replace the
landscape—and the heavens cannot be tempted to follow the lead of nature) a three-line catalogue beginning
and closing with the image of the ship, symbol of past
myths, leads into the final three-part negation. The
queen who is to be led with the accessory symbol of her
beauty ("conduisez la reine et son miroir") has in the
end neither ship, nor needle, nor mirror. The mission
is useless. The poem, which began with the lofty tone
and the signs of heroic gesture, falls on a complete
emptiness. There is finally no distinction between the
hero's action and the nonheroic gaze, when the landscape, which was to have been mythical (hence the
classic three sets of tripartite structures), becomes only
pathetic.

"As de Pique" (The Ace of Spades) contains a star-
tling combination of short verses, long prose para-
graphs, questions, statements made quietly or shouted
(TOUTES LES ÉTOILES SONT AU GIBET DEPUIS LA MORT DES
PLÉSIOSAURES/ ALL STARS HAVE BEEN ON THE GALLOWS
SINCE THE DEATH OF THE PLESIOSAURUSES), repetitions,

and diversions. The tone and the variations of rhythm are close to those of Blaise Cendrars, to whose poem on the dance there is a probable allusion in Péret's salute to a particular kind of adventure:

Et vive le vagabondage spécial[12]

(Long live the special wandering of a vagabond)

[12] See Blaise Cendrars, "Ma danse," of 1914, in *Du monde entier* (Gallimard, coll. Poésie, 1967), p. 81:

> Va-et-vient continuel
> Vagabondage spécial
> Tous les hommes, tous les pays
> C'est ainsi que tu n'es plus à charge
> Tu ne te fais plus sentir. . . .

And again, from Marinetti's *Initial Manifesto of Futurism* (February 20, 1909):

"Literature has hitherto glorified thoughtful immobility, ecstasy and sleep; we shall extol aggressive movement, feverish insomnia, the double-quick step, the somersault, the box on the ear, the fisticuff.

"We declare that the world's splendour has been enriched by a new beauty; the beauty of speed. A racing motor-car, its frame adorned with great pipes, like snakes with explosive breath . . . a roaring motor-car, which looks as though running on shrapnel, is more beautiful than the *Victory of Samothrace*.

"We shall sing of the man at the steering wheel, whose ideal stem transfixes the Earth, rushing over the circuit of her orbit." (Quoted Taylor, *op. cit.*, p. 124.)

For further comment on the sense of *dynamism*, see Gino Severini (quoted in Taylor, *op. cit.*, p. 11): "We choose to concentrate our attention on things in motion because our modern sensibility is particularly qualified to grasp the idea of speed. Heavy motorcars rushing through the streets of our cities, dancers reflected in the fairy ambiance of light and color, airplanes flying above the heads of the excited throng. . . . These sources of emotion satisfy our sense of a lyric and dramatic universe, better than . . . two pears and an apple."

For visual parallels to the poems and theories discussed here, compare Severini's canvas *The Train in the City*, 1914 (where the spirals of smoke and the angles of houses contrast with the

The whole poem itself is a movement, with the stated goal of seeing "eternal things." After questioning the chances of a renewed imagination ("Auras-tu la tête neuve?") the poet sets for himself a series of unlikely tasks, including the performance of alchemical transmutations ("Je changerai les métaux prisonniers des formes"), and of vanquishing kilometers already killed in order to arrive at tomorrow ("Et Demain/ DEMAIN"). The gestures are at once heroic, impossible, and imaginative, as the traditional burlesque or mock-epic coincides with the "lyric" comportment of surrealism:

Et personne ne passera plus sur la route. . . .
Je partirai à cheval sur des cervaux d'aliénés Et si je
ne vois personne je ferai des alligators avec tous les
animaux du chemin Je traînerai ma troupe en larmes
vers les cités paisibles et sur leur passage ce sera l'ère
des grands cataclysmes Si je vais sur l'océan je char-
merai tous les poissons. . . .

---

train's speeding straight line) with Cendrars' "Prose du Transsibérien." Compare Boccioni's spiral forms in his study for "Horizontal volumes," 1912, his *Spiral Composition* of 1913, and his
sculpture *Spiral Expansion* to Cendrars' praise of the spiraling
form, his *Elasticity* of 1912 (with its vaguely rubbery feeling)
to Cendrars' *Poemes élastiques*, and his *Dynamism of a Cyclist*,
1913, to the poem we are discussing. Carrà's *Woman at the
Window (Simultaneity)*, 1912, bears a clear likeness to the simultaneous poems, his *Jolts of a Cab*, 1911, to the surrealists' *beauté
convulsive*, and so on. To read Cendrars' poem for Delaunay's
La Tour without thinking of one of Delaunay's sixty Tower
paintings is to weaken the thrust of the poem, whose force lies
precisely in the dynamic relationship between the central up-
right form of the Eiffel Tower as it shoves aside all other elements in the poem, forcing them into a space newly emptied of
irrelevant details, and its pictured form, which controls in the
same way the other elements in the painting.

Je partirai Sept lieues d'un coup de pédale

Un grand bock d'espace s'il vous plaît
Anguille de route à rouler dans l'estomac (*GJ*, 73)

(And no one will ever pass down the road again. . . .
I shall go off on horseback over the lunatic brains
And if I see no one I shall make alligators from all
the animals on my way I shall drag my herd weeping
toward peaceful cities and on their passing it will be
the era of great cataclysms If I go over the ocean I
shall charm all the fish. . . .

I shall set off seven leagues with one stroke of the
pedal

A tall drink of space please
Eel of the winding road rolling in my stomach)

Yet once again all these beginnings of voyage—here
oddly juxtaposed, so that the road and the horse, the
ship and the bicycle are made interchangeable—end in
disaster. The heroic gesture takes on the self-deprecat-
ing air of charade, the "Manières de comédie," as the
hero suffers the indignities of mosquito bites, as well as
blows on the shin and the chest. Understandably, his
tone is more irritated than tragic:

Il est difficile de revenir sur ses pas comme les
tramways jusqu'à 1 2 1 1 1 1 1 1 1 2 2 2 2
ASSEZ (*GJ*, 76)

(It is hard to go back on your steps as trolleys
do up to 1 2 1 1 1 1 1 1 1 2 2 2 2
THAT'S ENOUGH)

However, the gesture is not to be predicted. A poem whose opening is far from epic in style and theme can end as if the whole voyage had been a noble one, conducted on the highest level of heroism and in the loftiest style. "Les Odeurs de l'amour" begins with the sort of extreme irrationality characteristic of the best-known surrealist gestures, with the pleasure of making love when one's body is tied up with thread and one's eyes closed by razor blades (an image as comforting as that of the razor slicing the eyeball in Bunuel's *Le Chien Andalou*). But then the woman loved comes forth accompanied by all the marks of majesty: her gaze travels before her, clearing the path, her hands upsetting the sky (here compared, perhaps because of its fluffy clouds, to an omelet), while flies expire all about her, owls take desperate flight, and a god is knocked from his ledge. Her body of the same color as the sun, she treads one of the most elevated paths physically possible:

Elle s'avance la bien-aimée aux seins de citron
Ses pieds s'égarent sur les toits (*GJ*, 120)

(She comes forth the beloved with lemon breasts
Her feet stray over the rooftops)

The vegetation rises from the earth to acclaim her as she unexpectedly dissolves entirely and magically in the cool air, before taking on once more her human shape. Even now, she is still touched by magic and violence— "Et ne sens-tu pas aussi que cette plante magique/ donne à tes yeux un regard de main/ sanglante/ épanouie" (And don't you feel also that this magic

plant/ lends your eyes a look of a bloody/ hand/ spread
out)—and still capable of upsetting all the forces of
nature through the strength of her tempestuous desire.
By her superhuman power, the poet loving her is also
lifted above the ordinary state, and together they enter
a marvelous state of perception where tempest merges
with noon. The brief final verse in the simplicity of its
vision is the fitting conclusion for the violent images of
this absurd but serious epic:

Je sais que le soleil
lointaine poussière
éclate comme un fruit mur
si tes reins roulent et tanguent
dans la tempête que tu désires
Mais qu'importe à nos initiales confondues
il est midi (*GJ*, 121)

(I know that the sun
faroff dust
bursts like a ripe fruit
if your intestines roll and sway
in the tempest you desire
But what does it matter to our entwined initials
it is noon)

This particular closing in brightness demonstrates the
perfect finality of an epic gesture, optically and emotion-
ally complete, or of an epic perception acknowledged.

Yet even in this clarity the epic is not literally comprehensible in our terms; it never occupies our own
space. The marvelous, which Péret compares to a time
bomb ready to burst forth, is characteristic of all times

and all places; but, he says, it cannot be clearly defined, since the sun tarnishes its peculiar brightness. It should only be, it can only be suggested. Nothing external can be compared to the explosion of the surrealist gesture, which is its own representation:

et le paysage n'est plus que le pôteau de lui-même

(and the landscape is from now on only the signal of itself)

THEORY AND INNER THEATRE

Let us leave to the schoolmasters the criticism of texts, to the esthetes the criticism of forms, and recognize that what has been said is not to be said again, that an expression is not valid twice, is not vital twice; that every word pronounced is dead and acts only in the moment when it is pronounced, that a form once used is no longer useful and can only lead to the search for another, and that the theatre is the only place in the world where a gesture made is not begun twice over.

> Artaud, *Le Théâtre et son double*

ARTAUD's statement unequivocally condemns our vocabulary, our perception, and our action, leaving no room for argument or objections. The negative weight of the central indictment is balanced, for those who would not so easily interrupt their interest in text, by the positive notes sounded at the beginning ("Let us," as if our cooperation in a revolutionary endeavor were invited) and at the conclusion, where the theatre is called "the only place." There is, then, some effort we might make and a place in which we might make it.

To write is to consume oneself, says Cendrars. Writing is the most dangerous, if the least rational, gesture, say the partisans of Dada; to the surrealists, words are at least as revolutionary as life, for whose renewal they are responsible. The word is not to be separated from the action, the violence or the novelty of the vocabulary from that of the deed. Benjamin Péret's *Grand jeu* is a game of language, and Bonnefoy's "Théâtre" is as linguistic as it is gestural. How then are we to separate text from theatre? Or, still more difficult, theory from gesture? In Bonnefoy's epic, which is a long poetic meditation on the problem of action, spectacle, and their cessation in the transfiguration of death, words are suddenly spotlighted in their singularity as is the unique gesture of an arm uplifted "through the ages." The spotlighting tends to halt the action contemplated, freezing it in a static frame which one could compare to a photograph, or to the petrification of the active play in the Kabuki theatre, where the monumental pose *mi-e* marks the climax of important scenes and epitomizes their character.[1] There is at this point no gulf dividing the lamentation and the celebration of language, between the particular word, text, or act and the generalizing of theatrical presentation.

But because the words are used up when uttered, and the forms burned out when once made explicit, the place where language and gesture meet is a tragic thea-

[1] As described by Rudolf Arnheim, *Visual Thinking* (University of California Press, 1969), p. 182.

tre, where the act is consumed in its doing. The brilliance of the spectacle depends on the violence of the motion from the vital to the exhausted gesture. A privileged position is given to the hero/poet acting out a role always unique, since it cannot be rehearsed, cannot be *repeated*, and incurs a terrible penalty even in its *re-presenting*.[2] In a dramatic universe where nothing can be assigned to a static position to be replayed, a particular value is conferred on the present. For the modern poet, says Bonnefoy, "this tree" has a meaning

[2] For a brilliant discussion of the theatre as it is menaced from within by its own "mal profond de la représentation," see Jacques Derrida, *De la grammatologie* (ed. Minuit, 1967, p. 430); elsewhere the same critic discusses at length the *initial repetition* of the gesture, the double origin of every linguistic act and its own essential repetition, so that a triadic concept is always at the base of *écriture* (Jacques Derrida, *L'Ecriture et la différence*, [Seuil, 1967]).

Compare Kandinsky's analysis of the union, within the *point*, of sound and silence, its repetition—"the absolute sound of the point"—and then "the sound of the given location in the basic plane," transforming the sound from absolute to relative. A point can produce a storm of sounds, starting with its own "inner sound," and the repetition of that sound, to the "double sound of the first point," and so on. The notion of the point itself implies energy and cruelty in just Artaud's sense: "The Point is the result of the initial collision of the tool with the material plane." (Wassily Kandinsky, *Point and Line to Plane*, tr. Hilla Rebay [Guggenheim Museum, 1947], p. 28.)

In "La Parole soufflée," an essay in *L'Ecriture et la différence*, Derrida also treats the particular complexity of Artaud's theories on the subject of written representation and its danger to the personality of the writer thus opened to the other's gaze, robbed of what is most valuable to him, word and breath: ". . . l'acte de lecture troue l'acte de parole ou d'écriture. Par ce trou j'échappe à moi-même. . . . La parole proférée ou inscrite, *la lettre*, est toujours volée. Toujours volée parce que toujours *ouverte*" (pp. 265-66).

greater than "tree," this single word a deeper resonance than the Word. The emphasis falls on the present tense and on the individuating adjective. Bonnefoy reminds us of Kierkegaard's remark that the Greek statue has no *look* because the Greeks, occupied only with the absolute, were unable to comprehend the present instant. By contrast, the contemporary poet and theoretician of poetry or theatre avoids at all cost the attitude of the statuesque. By his concentration on the present, he seeks to avoid the "sickness of representation" in so far as it applies to the eternal replaying of the same. Theatre and poetry, as we see them here, share a will to flux characterized by the images of unceasing motion, by the cultivation of metaphysical openness, and by the salute to the passing moment, respectively exemplified in the following chapters by the surrealists' choice of images in motion, Artaud's adaptation of Mexican mythology in its "open lines," and Bonnefoy's admiration for Baudelaire in his emphasis on mortality.

Yet, as we have seen before, the theoretical choice of the most violent and most continuous movement is no guarantee against the fall into the static or the stopped. The most rapidly moving circus is still composed of a basically unopened figure; the ring, after all, imprisons within a circular form.[3] Delaunay's profound deception with the cinema[4] resembles that of Artaud and the

---

[3] See also, in the next chapter, the circular surrealist poems, where the optimism at beginning again might be reversed by a simple movement of the mind to a despair at remaining in the same place.

[4] Robert Delaunay, *Du Cubisme à l'art abstrait: Documents inédits publiés par Pierre Francastel* (S.E.V.P.E.N., 1957), p.

surrealists: moving pictures are only pictures moving, the film is only a sequence of stills. The images of the most enthusiastic journeys may be transformed to those of the greatest stillness and the most anguishing *ennui*; the mind the most eager for present and passionate action may succumb to the most static despair; and the most fervent conviction in language as the continuing praise of the ephemeral instant may give way to the most irrevocable silence. The next three chapters treat of these situations as seen simultaneously in the language and the theory of the surrealist poets (where, for instance, the image of the venturing ship is succeeded by that of shipwreck), of Artaud (in whose writing the theatre of consummate motion and energy ends in paralysis and unmoving despair), and of Bonnefoy (whose poems as a moving theatre of the word make way finally for a painted picture of silence).

In their quieter tone, the texts to be examined in this second part will lead us, after the spectacle and the film, the circus and the game, toward a more inward and more theoretical path, toward what we have called the inner theatre of poetry.

229: "On ne peut pas créer la mobilité avec des choses dessinées, on ne peut pas créer la mobilité cinématique, parce que le cinéma n'est pas de la mobilité. Ce sont des images qui se font dans un temps très rapide. Ce n'est pas la mobilité."

A. *Motion and Motion Arrested: the Language of the Surrealist Adventure*

Nul grade, nul honneur dorénavant, n'excuseront
les jarrets raidis, les hanches soudées.

. . .

L'univers, saoûl, joyeux comme un bébé nègre ne
parle plus d'économiser ses forces.
Il s'en donne. Encore un verre d'oxygène.

. . .

Vive donc le bal musette.
Décidément c'est jour de fête.

René Crevel, *Renée Sintenis*

l'hypnotique paysage
le dramatique paysage
l'affreux paysage
le glacial paysage
l'absurde paysage blanc

Péret, *Dormir, dormir dans les pierres*

1. PERPETUAL MOTION

Within the surrealist gesture we sense a profound
ambiguity which lends a particular tone to all its manifestations in every field and in every theatre. To be sure,
the gesture points to itself always *in action,* the language abounds in terms of mobility, and the images
depend on constant and rapid metamorphosis. Even
Antonin Artaud, tragic and mentally immobilized, died
holding his shoe in his hand. To the surrealist imagina-

111

tion this is neither a cause for amusement nor a sign of insanity; it is, rather, significant of the continuing desire for adventure felt by every writer who has ever been connected with surrealism. That desire is in fact a defining quality of the surrealist attitude.

In 1969, some of the leading members of the Paris surrealist group rejected the label "surrealist," declaring an end to the limited period of particular or "historical" surrealism. The title of their new publication, *Coupure*, emphasizes a complete freedom from past styles of "surrealizing" and inaugurates a new epic of the marvelous. Poetry, in its truest sense, effects a necessary separation—or cutoff—between the poet and each successive landscape. Neither goals nor satisfaction can be reconciled with the true surrealist temperament or the genuine surrealist journey. In his praise of Eisenstein's film "The Battleship Potemkin," Robert Desnos perfectly describes the spirit of that journey: "It has weighed its anchor for good. It is on its way. Its wake embraces the world. Elements, frontiers, and men are powerless against it, and its invisible bowsprit shatters the sharpest reefs."[1] From the beginning, perpetual motion informs all possible perspectives on surrealism:[2] surrealism as a dynamics, surrealism by its violence resurrecting the static in an active mode. The experiments with language on which the original surrealist movement was based declare a revolution against all systems of petrification, an attack on the fixed. The demands

[1] Robert Desnos, *Cinéma* (Gallimard, 1966), p. 162.
[2] See, for instance, Louis Aragon, *Le Mouvement perpétuel* (Gallimard, 1925).

made on the surrealist word, freed of the ordinary restraints of logic and aesthetics, are moral ones. It must be a sufficient medium for the unrestrained exercise of the human imagination. Any concession to the flat realism of photographic representation is to be condemned according to the law of *becoming*, as any lapse into decorative facility is to be considered a betrayal of the liberating potential of the word. Surrealist language is not to be reduced to a means of communication like any other, is not be numbered among any group of other languages, whether living or dead.

The surrealist poet, able to perceive disturbances provoked by the visions of men even in the trajectories of stars, uses a constantly *changeable* discourse to translate these visions. Only mobile constellations of images can reflect his unconscious and highly mobile desires. Especially on the linguistic level, the temptation to inertia, the ordinary satisfaction with a specific pattern (the framework Desnos calls the FORMES-PRISONS) must be overcome, since the slightest immobility of form would impose on the changing transcriptions the unyielding rigidity of a statue or, worse, the dangerous illusion of the definitive. Thought and its transcriptions must not be allowed to solidify; the spontaneity of the marvelous must not be imprisoned.

All surrealist work, then, would seem to require an openness of form appropriate to the open and continuous vision the poet acts constantly to transcribe. Surrealist poems not only move in many directions simultaneously, but they also begin just at the moment when

113

they are ending. Caught within this deliberately circular language, or outside of it, the reader is never sure from what point of the circle or circumference the poet may be speaking, or to whom. All points are equally valid, and the circumference itself is extensible, the intentional equivalent of the semantic expansions in the serious experiments of surrealist word games. Here the circle does not limit nor is it limited.

Consider Guy Cabanel's poem on the alligator, a poem at once transparent and closed, a crystalline maze of verbal landscape. Beginning with the impressive statement, "Le seuil de glace ouvre sur le tragique dédale" (The threshold of ice leads to the tragic maze), it turns about a questioning of that statement, placed in the exact center of the poem: "Qui sait si le seuil de glace ouvre sur le tragique dédale" (who knows if . . .), and ends with a final restatement in the same words. The double circle of images where the maze is hidden under mirrors and mirages is reflected in the poetic form. But, again, each beginning or "seuil" opens another trajectory, another threshold and perspective. Cabanel's "Marabout" also begins with a waiting (as the surrealist attitude is properly *une attente*) and yet toward the completion of the circle, the waiting itself seems to be denied: "Il n'y a pas d'attente. . . ." (There is no waiting. . . .)[3] There may be no waiting because

[3] "Alligator" and "Marabout" from Guy Cabanel, *Maliduse* (St. Lizier, privately printed, 1961). The fact that Cabanel wrote the parts of his poems in a different order (see J. H. Matthews, *Surrealist Poetry in France* [Syracuse University Press, 1969]), does not in fact change the sequence in which we read them. Circles do not change their form because the gesture describing them starts in one or another place; see note 5 below on the cine-

the event has already taken place or, alternatively, because the action of awaiting is revealed as useless and illusory: no certain knowledge is possible.

2. ARRESTS AND FIXATIONS

But alongside the emphasis on free motion runs a parallel acknowledgment of necessity, to be seen on the theoretical, the thematic, and even the formal level of the work. In the periods of enthusiasm for automatic or spontaneous writing, the surrealist poet considers himself the transmitter of a message which *demands* transcription. Even when Aragon applies the phrase *Une Vague de rêves* to such transcription, which he sees as curved in form—a straight line would inhibit the flow of the marvelous, by its resemblance to the stiff contours of the everyday logic some call "reality"—he points out that this curved form is a *necessary* one. It is not far from the conception of necessity to that of stasis, from the idea of that which must be to that which cannot be changed. Even the circular poem, which may be considered a mobile conveyor of ambiguity (since it has no one direction outside itself), is not immune from the accusation of immobility. Again, the underlying ambiguity works in opposing senses. Breton's famous love poem on the sustained miracle of the marvelous, beginning and ending "Toujours pour la première fois" (Always for the first time), is ideally

matic loop. In this chapter, only the *trace* is examined, whereas in the chapters on Bonnefoy and Péret, it is the *gesture* which concerns us. "Le centre est le seuil"; in his essay on the elliptical form, Jacques Derrida analyzes this concept of the poet Jabès. (See "Ellipse," in *L'Ecriture et la différence*.)

115

circular in form and in concept;[4] it can be seen as the supreme example of the paradoxical surrealist voyage, both participating in the constant motion of the marvelous and revolving in the same place. The surrealist obsession with motion and with the mobility of language encourages a parallel obsession with the halt of language and with the static silence of things. The surrealist poem, for instance, is considered to occupy the same imaginative space as the surrealist film, making from a series of possibly disparate static perceptions or stills a continuous and moving unity; the surrealist language is a *cinema of the word*, where a succession of images is occasionally *stopped* by one of the still impressions.[5] The continuity and the interrup-

[4] In *L'Air de l'eau*, found in André Breton, *Poèmes* (Gallimard, 1948).

[5] But as Rudolf Arnheim points out in his *Art and Visual Perception: A Psychology of the Creative Eye* (University of California Press, 1954, 4th paper edn., 1969), "if a still picture is inserted in a film sequence, it will exhibit frozen motion rather than stillness" (p. 368). In this case, then, the flow of poetry prevents the image from conveying a static sense—it seems, rather, to be *suspended movement*.

Many of the techniques described in theories of art, photography, and film are of inestimable value in the analysis of surrealist poetry, as are the theories of other poetic movements. The chapters on "Movement" and "Tension" in the Arnheim study (where a protracted study is made of the oblique, of the deviations from restful attitudes in order to provide directed tensions and momentum) are especially instructive, as are various studies of *reversed* positions and *roughened* surface (see Renato Poggioli, *Poets of Russia, 1890-1930* [Harvard University Press, 1960], and Lemon and Reis, *Russian Formalist Criticism* [Nebraska University Press, 1965]), and of the oblique forms for which the Russian photographer and artist Rodzhenko is famous.

But film theory is of particular interest. For example, Moholy-

Nagy's idea of *simultaneous* screens or the *poly-cinema*, as he called it; Eisenstein's profoundly interesting contrast between the *mise-en-scène* and the *mise-en-cadre*, his notion of montage as necessary *collision* or *brilliant fusion* of images in their *super-impositions* (*The Film Sense*, Harcourt, Brace, 1942); and Stan Brakhage's homage to the loop machine as the creator of the perfect *cycle* whose beginning is indistinguishable from its termination (see note 3 above). These theories can all be applied in the *spatial* or/and in the *temporal* sense to the various perspectives which surrealist (and occasionally Dada) poets characteristically adopt in regard to the image. For the image can be simultaneously projected with another, or with itself (the realm of *poly-imagery* is often the realm of the surrealist marvelous); it can be created by collision or fusion with its polar opposite, or with elements irrelevant to it, and can, in its turn, collide or fuse with others. It can be superimposed, transparent, partly so, or opaque, on another image, so that all, some, or no parts of the other are in full evidence (in the latter case, still, the doubling changes the primary image). Two images can be merged, as a fitting form for the surrealist ideal of the "one in the other" I have discussed elsewhere (*The Poetry of Dada and Surrealism: Aragon, Breton, Tzara, Eluard, Desnos*, Princeton University Press, 1970); or one of a group of images can be circulated or cycled, alone or in succession with another series in such a fashion as to obliterate the boundary markings and emphasize the *flux*.

For those interested in theories of montage and in the instant telescoping of two different gestures, the fascination of oriental ideograms (a sort of "optical counterpoint," says Eisenstein in his *Film Form* [Harcourt, Brace, 1949]) is readily understandable. See Wylie Sypher, *From Rococo to Cubism in Art and Literature* (Random House, 1960), pp. 282-84, in the chapter "Camera and Cinema" for the technique of superposition as the key element in both Eisenstein's and Pound's appreciation of the ideograms.

Compare the futurist conception of superimposition as it is described in the *Technical Manifesto of Futurist Painting* (April 10, 1910), quoted in Taylor, *op. cit.*, p. 125: "How often have we not seen upon the cheek of the person with whom we were talking the horse which passes at the end of the street. Our bodies penetrate the sofas upon which we sit, and the sofas penetrate our bodies. The motor-bus rushes into the houses which it passes, and in their turn the houses throw themselves upon the motor-bus and are blended with it."

117

tions are more than interdependent; they are *intensifiers* each of the other. As in the canvasses of the early de Chirico, the profusion of trains, boats, and voyages is balanced by a contrary profusion of masks, mannequins, stopped clocks, and other such immobile crystallizations of movement. In Louis Aragon's *Le Paysan de Paris* (*The Peasant of Paris*), detailed menus, posters, and advertisements adorn the pages as if they were photographs hung on the wall, effectively halting the lyric flow of the descriptions; and in Crevel's *Êtes-vous fous?* (*Are You Mad?*) a series of recipes, formulas, visiting cards, multiplication tables, and lists of catastrophes appears only to mock the heroic pretensions of the novel's movement. In *La Liberté ou l'amour!* (*Liberty or Love!*) by Robert Desnos, a gigantic and smiling figure observes all the action from the motionless vantage point of a billboard, in the place of any less reliable and more changeable living observer. During the central love scene, the reader's attention is suddenly drawn to the calendar fixed on the hotel wall as it arrests time and, with it, human freedom of action. (In this particular context, the two potentially synonymous terms of *La Liberté ou l'amour!* seem oddly opposed, as if one had to choose between freedom from time and the eternal yet time-bound slavery to passion.) Similarly, in Desnos' early poems, the formal and thematic progression may be interrupted by a sudden focusing on one object of the poet's gaze, for example, on the way in which the woman's hair is *fixed* with a comb, as if this point in the landscape had become an obsession stemming the current of the poem. But, in fact, these recurring points of reference serve as centers of reserved energy, from which the momentum of the word starts out continually renewed, "Toujours pour la première fois." This *holding* in turn acts as the focus for the linguistic movement and the guarantee of its poetic force, since the obsessive images take on the proportions of a myth together with its generative grandeur.

Again, a specific and significant perception can be taken as exemplary of surrealist vision, a specific poem as a model of surrealist poetry; this procedure, expansive rather than reductive, is appropriate to the spirit of surrealism. But the film can be shown again and again, as the poem on the page can be reread. Are they each fixed, the surrealist film on celluloid, the surrealist poem on the page, and the significant or startling image within the surrealist poem? Are they all threatened with becoming mere monuments to a talent, to a moral and imaginative commitment, or to a historical moment from which a separation must eventually be made? Is surrealism to be considered just another literary attitude, with its documents, its historians, and its commentators?

3. Sightlessness and Shipwreck

The crisis of the object detected by the surrealist poet in our present "era of metamorphosis" may soften all material profiles considerably, enabling certain of these objects to enter into a necessary communication with our desire, but too clear a vision is apt to retard the interior, unfocused drift of the imagination. Daytime vision is less open to rapid metamorphosis than is the vision behind closed eyes, for dream is clearly more suited to the surrealist adventure. Thus the surrealist trip, unlike ordinary intellectual or touristic experiences, is often described as sightless. So Alain Jouffroy calls himself a blind explorer, and Robert Benayoun completes a poem with the promise: "Et les yeux une bonne fois clos nous partirons."[6] A privileged landscape but more of desire than of possession, a conveyor of passion rather than of rest, the bed is, as often as the ship, identified with the adventure of writing itself. Moreover, at the point when a ship might become a useless vessel, surrounded by soluble fish, the bed still hurtles along on its wheels of blue honey,[7] crashing through all the stop signals like the surrealist sentence on which one can set no limits of speed or space.

No complacent *regard* of the canvas or of the cinematic stills or even of the position of the poem on the particular page is permitted to the surrealist traveler, who risks no limit to his possibility of a mobile consciousness. Obsessions are translated into recurring themes and images, but those images are not to be contemplated as ends in themselves: the surrealist voyage is supposed to be endless. Contemplation suits the realm of the aesthete, not that of the surrealist, which refuses any aestheticism as an acceptance of the inactive, as a paralysis of passion. Furthermore, the widest

[6] The concluding line of "Perception de la ligne droite," in J. H. Matthews, ed., *An Anthology of French Surrealist Poetry* (University of Minnesota Press, 1966).

[7] See André Breton, "Fata Morgana," found in *Poèmes*; see also Robert Desnos, "The Night of Loveless Nights," found in *Domaine public* (Gallimard, 1953).

vision of the world beyond the canvas, beyond the circus of Dada and the cinema of surrealism, is still a limiting one. Ironically, it is in an essay on the melancholy of the cinema that Desnos admits: "The doors which we open lead to pitiful landscapes, and close on other pitiful landscapes."[8] To the bed, as to the ship, the certainty of a permanent voyage or of a marvelous vision cannot be guaranteed.

Surrealist language is not always simple, and the surrealist attitude is almost always ambiguous. The dialectical nature of the surrealist approach determines the form of such double images as the machine whose workings Breton wishes to *paralyze* in water, the train *stopped* at full speed in a deserted countryside or in a virgin forest or whose motion is swallowed up in ivy tentacles (images mentioned by Leiris, by Breton, and by Péret), and a bird of flight plummeting to earth, as in the poetry of Tzara, or *transfixed* by its own wings, as in that of Eluard. The language of surrealism is, like beauty, convulsive; it is also an *explosante-fixe*. Surrealist mobility cannot be inscribed within an unambiguous one-element system, cannot even be characterized by a single attribute. Its motion is forever balanced and intensified by the cessation of motion.

For Dada, the crystal is movement in all its purity, and the crystal mountains, like the corridors of glass, favor rapidity of action and clarity of gesture. For surrealism, the crystal is the perfect, impossible, and therefore marvelous material of which houses, poems, and lives should be built, partly for its transparency and

---

[8] Robert Desnos, *Cinéma*, p. 175.

partly because it represents motion stopped at its highest point. But Breton imagines himself to be finally caught, like Theseus, within his labyrinth of crystal. Aragon is a willing prisoner of the dizzying maze created by the curve of language. Even the adventuring ship of Robert Desnos, as much a galley of love as a free agent of the surrealist vision, is finally trapped, like Apollinaire's, in the crystalline ice floes, another tragic maze. Desnos himself, once acknowledged to be the most successful experimenter with sleep writing, is at last as conscious of the paper on which he writes, of the ink molecules and the film of moisture before the reader's eye, as of the adventures he elaborates. At a given moment, perhaps inevitably, the crystal loses its transparency to become a simple reflector. Narcissus, warns Crevel, was caught in a petrifying fountain. The sea of adventure is changed, at some point, into the desert where the poet can see only his own image, while the endless pilgrimage of motion becomes a looking-glass mirage. In a poem of experimental language, Desnos suddenly exclaims:

Eh quoi déjà je miroir.[9]

(Well already I mirror)

The hero of openness is now the victim of shipwreck. And yet shipwreck is as essential to the surrealist ad-

[9] "Idéale maîtresse," in "Langage cuit," from *Domaine public.* Compare "Le désert qui s'étendait autour de moi était peuplé d'échos qui me mirent cruellement en présence de ma propre image reflétée dans le miroir des mirages," from "L'Aumonyme," in *Domaine public*, p. 56.

venture as is the sea. Aragon describes the surrealist group's hurling itself into the *Vague de rêves* (*Wave of dreams*) of automatic writing as the waves threaten to carry them out to the domain of the sharks of madness; in fact the copy of the book he gave to Eluard is inscribed to his partner in shipwreck ("ami de naufrage"). Desnos confesses his hope that the ship of which he has been fondest may be wrecked some day. He has longed for the shipwreck, for the ice floes, for the impossibility included in every surrealist possibility, and for the eventual end of dreaming implied in the conception of the surrealist dream. He poses a question to which he knows the answer to be already given:

> . . . la nuit
> Naufrage la nuit?[10]

> (. . . night
> Shipwrecks night?)

The time and the place of adventure may serve to undermine the force of that adventure; again, its own intensity may be proved by its self-destructive thrust, its initial undetermined mobility, magnified in retrospect by the sudden immobilization it chooses and inflicts.

4. The Open Movement

At the conclusion of Crevel's major novel, *Êtes-vous fous?*, the bed which had been a ship of fever writing its mad dance upon the sky throughout the night is

---

[10] "Sirène-Anémone," in *ibid.*

finally wrecked. In this last dawn, a pathetic parallel to the dawn on which the novel opened and another affirmation of the circular voyage, Crevel admits that he has not been able to carry his idea to its flamboyant limits. And he laments the cessation of all adventure on a heroic scale. To himself in the person of the shipwrecked voyager, he cries: "Immobile will be your path. . . ."[11] Resolving to ask for no help, to make no signal to the ghost ships that pass, he permits himself only to ask one question. With that question the motion of the book ends, the voluntary verbal prefiguration of the novelist's own suicide, and still continues beyond its own space in a difficult, necessarily unresolved form:

Êtes-vous fous?
Si non . . .[12]

(Are you mad?
If not . . .)

The opening left by that unanswered question is sufficient for any answer and any further series of ambiguities. The surrealist language cannot be limited to the well-defined space occupied by the clear responses of ordinary language or to the problems elucidated by all forms traditional and transfixed.

To the uninitiated, the apparent halt to adventure may seem a contradiction of the vertigo essential in surrealism, a concession to the *immobilisme* Breton fought against all his life, and a betrayal of the vow taken by

[11] Rene Crevel, *Êtes-vous fous?* (Gallimard, 1929), p. 178.
[12] *Ibid.*, p. 179.

Crevel and the other surrealists to work for the end of the Motionless. But Guy Cabanel reminds us in his "Point d'équilibre" that the most rapidly spinning wheel may seem not to be moving at all. Only those participating in the surrealist attitude could ever properly describe its ambiguous reversals, telling us at what point the maze is a crystal and the ice floes the open sea. What seems to be a shipwreck may be only the exterior sign of a voyage beyond the distinction both of motion and of nonmotion, toward the specific linguistic gesture of the most genuine *surrealist movement*.

B. *Artaud's Myth of Motion*

> . . . la chute mince et ralentie de l'esprit.
>
> *Le Pèse-Nerfs*

> L'horrible, Madame, est dans
> l'immobilité de ces murs,
> de ces choses. . . .
>
> "Lettre à la voyante," *L'Art et la mort*

Of all the ambiguous reflections on movement and on its tragic cessation, that of Artaud is the most complex and the most theatrically engaging. To follow the track of his gesture is to trace the steps of a specifically surrealist genius. Here the role of heroic actor becomes indistinguishable from the roles of creator and spectator of action or paralysis, and those latter roles become indistinguishable. The multiple becomes singular, and the singular, double: that is to say, the notion of theatre becomes that of the Theatre and its *double*,[1] while the action and the vision, the passion and the word, coalesce.

1. A SPASMODIC THEATRE

Artaud, like the surrealists Breton and Péret, was strongly attracted to Mexican folklore, in which they all saw a manifestation of the peculiarly unitary quality of the Mexican mind. The firm denial of any split between logic and irrationality, reason and imagination, or between the objective and the subjective is natural to the Mexican people, according to Benjamin Péret,[2] who describes this poetic attitude as being in open conflict with the practical necessities of modern life and with our ordinary vocabulary, and as being an excellent example of the surviving mental state which can serve to generate the myth.

Artaud's admiration for Mexican mythology is, as he explains in *Le Théâtre et les dieux*, based on its recognition of movement as the essential character of human thought in its contacts with the world. This mythology of motion he calls an "open" mythology;[3] the Mexican landscape and traditional Mexican art are full of open forms, he says, and the Mexican gods have open contours, signaling both departure and return. From this,

[1] *Oeuvres complètes* (Gallimard, 1961), I, 273. References to this work will be made by volume number in the text.

[2] Benjamin Péret, *Anthologie des mythes, légendes et contes d'Amérique* (Albin Michel, 1960), p. 33; see also his vivid presentation of *Le Livre de Chilam Balam de Chumayel* (Denoël, 1955).

[3] *Les Tarahumaras* (Décines, 1963), p. 207. Referred to in the text as *T*.

man can learn a pattern of thinking which will enable him to come out of himself, to move beyond his psychologically fixed or closed situation. In a rhythm that Artaud sees as geometrically active, human thought moves from the dead point of abstract emptiness at the center of things out toward the concrete world of color and events. To follow this rhythm suggested by the Mexican landscape and traditions is to involve oneself in the occult which is nevertheless on the surface of life itself, to participate in the cruelty of living instead of in the passivity of mere existence, to act at once in death and in life through a difficult metaphysical discipline, in an aesthetic, psychological, and spiritual necessity. This he calls *culture*, and it is the essential basis of theatre: "Culture is a movement of spirit from emptiness toward forms, and from forms toward emptiness, as toward death. To be cultivated is to consume forms, burning them up in order to live. It is learning to hold oneself erect in the incessant movement of forms which are destroyed one after the other." (*T*, 203) The action of theatre is thus a coming and going between death and life. Artaud discusses at some length how the fear of the empty center acts as a motor for the outward motion toward the world of fullness and forms, how the theatrical burning of exterior forms releases the energy for the motion back to the center. Gesture, or the double of thought in the realm of matter, he explains as the concrete realization of the dynamics of leaving and returning in a continuous staging. Although the act of writing can, by its lack of movement, stifle the "vast breathing" of the spirit in a silent crystallization, Artaud

127

says that his theatre corresponds exactly to the image of a sound, absorbing and reflecting within itself all the noise and movement of life. Like the spasmodic civilization he sees in Mexico and in direct opposition to the vain estheticism of a lifeless and closed art—an art that bears reference only to its own gratuitous surface of forms, language, and appearance, with no dynamic gesture pointing beyond the sign to the reality signified—Artaud's theatre of thought is a theatre of mobility, depending on an open rhythm, necessary and therefore cruel, as Artaud uses the word. Thus, after the basic correspondences and laws of harmony have been perceived, the "gratuitous and useless gesture is placed in its useful setting, relative to the principal laws," the exercise of law being the inescapable source of energy. (*IV*, 312)

The final goal of Artaud's theatre is, like that of the games of antiquity, "this knowledge which dominates destiny by action." What must be known is the totality of nature, as it is set to the rhythm of human thought, and conversely in man, his consciousness set to the rhythm of events." (*T*, 194) This complete and active interpenetration makes up the reality which must be represented in the theatrical gesture taken as the exterior manifestation of thought. To the progress of thought Artaud applies a series of highly active descriptions. It is cruelty, intensity, action, presence of life, conflict of adverse forces; it is vigorous, energetic, and bloody. And conversely, his descriptions of gesture appear indeed at first sight more appropriate to thought than to action: it is bare, pure, essential, precious, rare, precise, intellectual, and of a quintessence and a necessity that are absolute. These unexpected switches of vocabulary are an important indication of the intermingling of categories Artaud insists on, in accordance with his ideal mobility of thought in all its openness of line. Both of these traits, as we have seen, are characteristics he perceives in Mexican thought; the fact that he perceives them is for us more significant than the decision as to whether or not they are in fact characteristic of that thought.

Artaud's theatre is also a *théâtre par la poésie*, a theatre by means of poetry. He defines poetry as a special sort of knowledge, that of the internal and dynamic workings of thought itself, or, again, as the translation into action of the most extreme ideas. (*III*, 241) While the alchemical or poetic theatre attempts to construct an "edifice of movement" in the objective world where motion is easily grasped, it must at the same time "interiorize" the actor's playing, in strict accordance with the interior and necessary movement of thought. (*III*, 120, 277) This theatre replaces the classic theatre of individual psychological motivation where feeling is studied as an inert and lifeless object of photography. (*III*, 216) A good example of "closed" art, psychological theatre is totally anti-heroic and devoid of action, says Artaud; the reality it presents is desolate and flat, suggestive of no value beyond itself. He shares the Pirandellian conception of man as a scattered and many-sided being in a room of mirrors, and demands a theatre of movements sufficiently diverse in their meaning and their presentation to convey human complexity. (*III*, 216) For this reason, it is not surprising that his objections to the staging of certain plays (such as Passeur's *Les Tricheurs* and Bruckner's *Mal de la jeunesse*) are based on their immobile quality. Artaud insists above all on the enlarging function of the theatre, which must open out beyond the narrow limits we often set for it. This is his basis for refusing the purely verbal theatre of the West, which arrests thought, inhibits psychological insight, and paralyzes the gesture. "For even from the Western point of view it must be admitted that the word has ossified, that all words have congealed, have become glued to their meanings in a schematic and limited terminology." (*IV*, 141)

We can easily see, therefore, why Artaud should have been so enthusiastic about the silent cinema. In the 1920s he had found its mobile structure far more promising than that of the theatre because it more skillfully created an atmosphere of mystery, revealing the secret transformations of the interior self and blurring the usual clarity that paralyzes the life of the spirit. In the ideal film human psychology would be devoured by the dynamics of action, and film in general should have been the perfect successor to the outmoded theatre. But in the 1930s Artaud became disillusioned with the cinema; in his view, the addition of sound disrupts the flow of images in their implications and extensions. In a scathing article of 1933 entitled "The Early Aging of the Cinema," he says that films supply us with an instant diet, fragmentary and facile, their order relating only to certain exterior habits of vision and memory, their formal technique limited to the representation of an accidental and incomplete world, finite and desiccated.[4] If the world we are shown is not the unitary and open one Artaud takes as his beginning point, it is the fault of the medium. Since the film-maker's choice is not spontaneous but is, Artaud thinks, generally made before the moment of presentation, the gesture is given to us as *already perfected*, leaving no place for the mobilizing influence of the human mind. "The world of the cinema is a closed world, bearing no relation to existence." (*III*, 98) Frozen, or glued, into immobility, lacking any possibility of change or becoming, the structure of the cinema is not parallel to the active structure of thought or to the laws of reality, which Artaud always sees as closely related to thought. Since it cannot present real objects or enter the movement of life, "the film is a dead world, unrelated and full of illusion." (*III*, 97) Cut off from action and expansion, it can go no further than a kind of excitation of the nerves. "Because it is empty of depth, of density, of distance and of interior motion, we cannot hope that it will represent the Myth of modern life." (*II*, 99) After this disappointment, Artaud is forced to confine all his hope for the restoration of Myths to his idea of the theatre.

2. CONTINUITY AND PARALYSIS

But the unitary basis Artaud always insists on threatens even his conception of the mythic theatre. "For more and more life will become inseparable from spirit";

---

[4] The chief distinction he makes between his own film *La Coquille et le clergyman* and other surrealist films is that while the latter are gratuitous in their action, his scenario is based on a necessary flow of images.

(*III,* 81) he clings to the principle of a mobile continuity between language and reality, mind and the works of the mind, and between the stages of personality that individual works manifest. In *L'Ombilic des limbes* he attacks the separations usually made between these elements for provoking a reduction of the person, a scission of possible vitality. Of his own writing he says that it must be "bitten" by external things, by all the moments to come. (*I,* 49) His refusal to distinguish between temporary states in the world and in himself is, in so far as we can judge, genuine and must be taken into account in any discussion of his work. If Artaud sees his individual anguish as inseparable from his poetic and theoretical productions, these productions should not be, though they often are, considered in isolation from his personality. Such an attitude he might have characterized as a closed criticism, partial and discontinuous and therefore of necessity insignificant as well as immobile.

Artaud's sickness, which he refers to as "The poison of being. A true paralysis," (*I,* 40) is graver and more difficult than a purely metaphysical or psychological limitation would be. When he calls this a physical and almost exterior anguish and thus distinguishes it from the anguish characteristic of the other writers of his time,[5] he is calling attention to the totality of his own

---

[5] In a letter of 1924 Artaud explains to Jacques Rivière that the leaps and sudden stops in his poetry are the result of his mental inability to concentrate on any object, a weakness he calls typical of the age and of other poets such as Reverdy, Breton, and Tzara. But he goes on to say that for them the weakness touches only the area of thought, whereas for him it is physi-

sickness and to its permanence; the only possible escapes from it, he says, are in complete madness or in the grave. A metaphysical paralysis or temporary absence of the mind could be overcome by action in the objective exterior world, whereas this all-penetrating paralysis has no solution on either the exterior or the interior level. It is, of course, an ironically fitting illness for a man who depends so heavily on the unity of levels. The sickness affects his being in all its representations: that he should be so conscious of it is doubly pathetic in view of his repeated insistence on motion, energy, purity, continuity, and presence:

> I have no life, I have no life! My interior effervescence is dead. . . . Try to understand. It is not even a question of the quality of images, of the quantity of thought. It is a question of sparkling VIVACITY, of truth, of reality. There is no more life. . . . I cannot think. Understand this hollowness, this intense and durable nothingness. . . . I can go neither forward nor backward. I am transfixed, localized at the same point. . . . My thought is no longer developing in space, nor in time. I am nothing. I have no being. . . . I am not there. I am no longer there, and this will last forever. (*I*, 298-300)

It may be argued that in Artaud it is hard to determine the exact proportion of pose, to separate voluntary dramatics from genuine feeling. But the recurrence

---

cal, constant, and all-pervading: "Cette inapplication à l'objet qui caractérise toute la littérature, est chez moi une inapplication à la vie. Je puis dire, moi, vraiment, que je ne suis pas au monde, et ce n'est pas une simple attitude d'esprit" (ɪ, 39).

of particular terms and patterns of feeling must be seen as significant of his preoccupations, whose peculiarly unfruitful and incommunicable nature he laments. The very passages confessing his repetitive, limited vocabulary are those which reach us with the greatest clarity:

> I believe I have bored people long enough with the account of my spiritual poverty, my atrociously threadbare psyche, and I think they have the right to expect more from me than lamentations of my impotence and enumerations of impossibilities, or otherwise I should be quiet. But the problem is precisely that I am alive. (*I*, 273)

Since one of the primary determinations of *l'être* as Artaud defines it is expansion and mobility of thought, he believes any reduction of this mobility to be a reduction in essence. In one letter of 1929 he complains of being *arrested* in a literal sense, and in another, of being forced to undergo an evil "spell of disorder, impotence, incoherence." (*III*, 148, 178)[6] When writing to Paulhan describing the interior battle his mind rarely wins, the adjectives he applies to his sickness suggest an immobility in both the physical and mental realms: "enlisé," "ligoté." (*III*, 272) And in letters to Dr. Allendy about his intellectual vacuum and his intense ennui, Artaud finds that his thought has neither extension nor continuity, that his stuttering speech is paralleled by the contraction of his thinking, which "hardens" and

---

[6] Artaud, always conscious of the dangers of pose discussed above, calls these feelings a phony romanticism and struggles against them with an effort that cannot be interpreted as insincere.

then stops altogether. Certain as he is of the necessary union of outward form and inward reality, he sees these patterns of paralysis as linked to the same problem of immobility which he hoped to overcome through his theatre. In this perspective what might otherwise seem trivial takes on an entirely different appearance. We have no choice but to accept Artaud's intentions as to the interpenetration of mind and work and to listen to his own warning: "The true exercise of the spirit undermines life like a sickness." (*IV*, 286)

This does not simply mean that the Theatre can be compared to the Plague. If life is essentially the "progress of thought," then the malady attacking thought threatens life at its root and, with it, the notion of the theatre Artaud so intimately connects with life and above all with thought. The structure of the metaphysical or theatrical connection between the abstract center of emptiness and the world full of forms cannot be sustained when the possibility for the individual to act is sapped or when the movement of the mind comes to a stop. If thought lacks the energy to "consume the forms" it will not push beyond the formal surface, and the theatre may become as ineffectual and its representation as incomplete as the cinema. The edifice of motion cannot be built on an immobile structure or an inactive imagination: "The real object of the theatre is the creation of Myths. . . ." (*IV*, 139) If the signs and the gesture lose their expansion or if the pure mobility is paralyzed, then the mythic theatre becomes in its turn a closed art and an outworn myth. Artaud's conception of the theatre, if it is connected as closely to his thought

135

as he intended, is endangered by his own sickness—a destiny he was unable to dominate even through knowledge. His lament in *Les Tarahumaras* should not be forgotten: "For the danger of myths, no matter how noble and how tenacious, is that they burn out." (*T*, 163)

3. THE TRAGIC PLACE

"Life will create itself, events unfold, spiritual conflicts be resolved, and I will not share in it." (*I*, 113) Condemned to the position of spectator ("à côté de la vie"), the Artaud of *L'Ombilic des limbes* and *Le Pèse-Nerfs* feels himself to have grown imbecilic from the anguish of his thoughts deformed and suppressed, "vacant from the stupefaction of my tongue." (*I*, 92) No matter how his mind turns to a place beyond this paralysis, toward an AILLEURS, his own vocabulary ("mes termes"—where, obsessed, he sees only endings: "une suite de terminaisons") forces upon him the localization he most dreads. The man who does not smell of "la bombe cuite" and vertigo is not worthy to be alive, he says in his essay "Van Gogh suicidé par la société." "And life should be lived." (*I*, 101)

The notion of suspension haunts the sick consciousness. If life is a series of appetites, contradictions, temptations good and bad, Artaud will make himself a deliberate prey of circumstances and thereby participate, however passively, in them from his circumscribed and terrible place ("ce lieu menaçant, ce lieu terrassant") of suspended sensitivity. (*I*, 90) "I put myself in suspension, uninclined, neutral." (*Bilboquet*, *I*, 222) Replacing all the desperate efforts of self-awareness and the consummation of thought ("Je me pense"), he will concentrate on the most unconscious reaches of his own being ("les ramifications les plus *impensées*") to experience the laws which determine him in his motionless state, the opposite of the ideal and active condition he described in *Le Pèse-Nerfs* ("se retrouver dans un état d'extrême secousse." *I*, 88) He is the eternal witness of himself, the only spectator of his own pathetic internal theatre of despair, which he judges to be a universal one: "I can neither die nor live, nor desire to die or to live. And all men are like me." (*I*, 223)

But in "L'Enclume des forces" (in *La Révolution surréaliste*, no. 8, 1926), the endless natural gyrating motion of the stars (associated with the laws of nature Artaud takes as the necessary setting for the theatrical gesture, otherwise confined to the realm of the gratuitous) makes the sight of a lone and motionless object all the more vivid: "An idea of the desert hangs over these summits, above which floats a comet,[7] horribly, inexplicably suspended." (*I*, 142) All men may indeed, by their condition, be condemned to a place of inaction and a theatre of non-desire; nevertheless, an heroic effort, even if it is no longer expressed in an epic vocabulary, may stand out like the comet among the stars.

Another essay in *L'Art et la mort* pays a double hom-

---

[7] This "astre échevelé" ("star with disheveled hair"), betrays Artaud's own obsession with hair, as well as that of his mental counterpart, Uccello (discussion below). See, in the poem "La Nuit opère" from *Bilboquet*, the horror of the poet who feels his hair "grandir et se multiplier." (I, 227)

age to the heroic gesture and to the extraordinary complexity of the apparently trivial. "Uccello le poil" is a remarkable description of the painter Paolo Uccello, above whose immense and heavy[8] head the whole universe hangs, "strangled, and suspended, and eternally vacillating." And yet what Uccello contemplates, "wrapped in his beard," and Artaud with him, is the immense shadow of one hair, its relation to forests, eyelashes, grass, veins, wrinkles, shoelaces, the line, the tongue, and the sign. He lives in this idea of *depth* as in a living poison, turning eternally in its circles. Artaud, seeing himself deprived of any relation to "earth," praises Uccello for his "earthy and rocky preoccupation with depth." He hovers over the abysses of madness from which he is removed by the distance of one hair, a space still sufficient to save him forever, and as a hero, if only he makes the gesture: "Wash, wash your lashes, Uccello, wash the lines, wash the trembling trace of hairs and wrinkles . . . and in your monstrous palm . . . there appears once more the august trace of your hair emerging with its delicate lines like the dreams of your drowned-man's brain." (*I*, 139) Damned with a spirit as hollow as Artaud's own,[9] he has nevertheless been able

---

[8] The adjectives "plate" and "lourde" may refer to the attractive awkwardness of the unmodeled and unshaded surface of the paintings of Uccello, where, for instance, a crowd of horses all seem to stand on the same vertical line, each above the other, their eyes the main points of focus and perspective in relation to the onlooker.

[9] Artaud writes several notes on Uccello, whose person he can assume in the *strictest* sense, by his will to a loss of personal liberty: "J'ai tenté la fusion avec le mythe de Paolo Uccello. Je me

to make his universe from the infinitesimally small ("a smaller thing even than the trace and the beginning of an eyelash"). The lesson he teaches is one of silence and of satisfaction in the motionless, with less even than a place—a single line,[10] and that "impalpable." As Artaud says in another meditation on Uccello:

---

cantonne dans le mythe. Je suis vraiment Paul les Oiseaux. Mon esprit ne peut plus tenter le moindre écart à droite, à gauche." This essentially theatrical changing of roles is based on a tragic psychological similarity: "Paolo Uccello est en train de se débattre au milieu d'un vaste tissu mental où il a perdu toutes les routes de son âme et jusqu'à la forme et à la suspension de sa réalité." (I, 55) And finally, as Artaud takes upon himself the *myth* of UCCELLO, the historical and *given* name, this name "dont on l'appelait" is transformed into its French form, freely chosen and signifying the painter's rebirth in the person of Artaud.

[10] But the concept of line implies more movement than we would ordinarily expect. For the Gestalt psychologists, it implies tension between centers of forces, charges in an electromagnetic field, as Stephen Pepper explains in his chapter, "Line" in *Principles of Art Appreciation* (Harcourt, Brace, 1949). And for kinesthetic theoreticians, says Pepper, "line is felt wherever the body moves." The movement of the eye forms the basis of visual line, the movements of other parts of the body that of lines perceived or *felt* in other ways: lines are, for these theoreticians, *dimensions* and *directions*. (Of particular interest for the problem of discontinuous and temporarily stilled motion discussed above in connection with the cinema is Pepper's observation that the "curved line is perceived through a series of jerky movements," p. 176.)

Wassily Kandinsky, for whom the simple point demonstrates the coincidence of extreme inner or concentric tension with extreme restraint ("the briefest, constant, innermost assertion"), describes the pushing of the point into the line by an outside force in a highly energetic terminology: "This force hurls itself upon the point which is digging its way into the surface, tears it out and pushes it about on the surface in one direction or another." The line "is created by movement—specifically, through the destruction of the intense self-contained repose of the point.

Two or three signs in the air, what man could pretend to live more than those three signs, and of whom, in the space of the hours hanging over him would one imagine requiring more than the silence preceding them or the phosphorous of space dragged along by my passing as they make their way through me. They form words of one black syllable in the meadows of my brain. Uccello, you teach us how to be no more than a line and the elevated place of a secret. (*I*, 140)

The gesture paralyzed, the mind obsessed, the thought reduced are not necessarily the signals of despair. The tragic place, menacing to our sanity, victorious over our strongest urge to motion, can serve still as the place of heroic theatre just when we, and the actor suddenly changed to hero, would least have expected it. "Did you foresee my descent into this world below with my mouth open and my spirit perpetually astonished? Did you foresee these cries in all the directions of the world and of language, like a spool frenetically unwound?" (*I*, 140)

Here, the leap out of the static into the dynamic occurs." The straight line represents, in its tension, "the most concise form of the potentiality for endless movement." (*Point and Line to Plane*, tr. Hilla Rebay [Guggenheim Museum, 1947], pp. 32, 54, 57.) It would probably be unwise, therefore, to take Artaud's celebration of the line as a eulogy of the most minimal arts: in its tension, whether we see it or not, there may be a whole *play* of energy.

C. *Yves Bonnefoy: Not the Peacock but the Stone*

Je suis venu au théâtre des pierres.

Le Coeur-espace

The final place is reserved for Bonnefoy's timeless meditations on what might be called universal qualities, on the abstract ideas of motion and immobility as they are reflected in and then superseded by the dual tragic gesture, in the passing, imperfect moment which redeems the fault of perfection. Here the frantic motion of circus, cinema, and theatre is reduced to a pool of color, or to one painting. Artaud saves himself and us by a contemplation of one line; Bonnefoy saves the passing moment by the contemplation of one leaf and of one poem arrested on a page, the mobile by what is more passing than permanent.

1. NAMING AND UNITY

In the art of Byzantium pictured by a certain turn-of-the-century sensitivity as the art of the immobile and the absolute negation of the senses, Bonnefoy sees rather an infinite consuming of existence by whatever means possible, most particularly the voyage. "Let a ship sail from a port by night and the Byzantium of the spirit shone already like another riverbank."[1] All the diverse forms constituting its *appel*—in the strongest sense of appeal, almost a summons—are indications of "existence attempted," of the finite made present, and

[1] "Byzance," *Un Rêve fait à Mantoue* (Mercure de France, 1967), p. 11.

141

yet they incarnate the eternal freedom of Desire and Knowing, infinitely preferable to the lowly attachments of tangible Possession.

That preference, which Bonnefoy distinguishes in most of the artists of the present, is exemplified in the paintings of Miró, where the act of understanding (*comprendre*) is stressed above the act of taking or acquiring (*prendre*).[2] Value is attached not to the object as a static thing-in-itself, but to the gesture by which it is to be investigated, not to the painted surface of reality but to the act of painting. Miró does not copy the greenery; rather, he takes the green from his tube of color. Bonnefoy's attitude toward art in no way entails any false claims for the scope of the artistic gesture, since he sees the work of art as a "limited action" at best. Seeing and making seen (in Eluard's terminology) are not the real point. Spectacle is secondary to a deeper interior contemplation. For the present state of things, for our conventional morality, the artist substitutes a "*fluidity* where sensation and imagination enrich each other"; for the unity of the object seen in a classic art, he substitutes the unity of an elemental and universal consciousness latent in our desire, (*M*, 16) and in place of the natural urge to repose or to happiness, he recommends the constant psychological activity of unrest itself.

How then, in the important essay on the "Act and

[2] *Miró* (Milan, Silvana, 1964), p. 26. Bonnefoy elaborates later in the essay: "atténuer l'esprit de possession personnelle . . . spiritualiser son désir de prendre . . . remonter, peu à peu, à travers les choses vers l'unité."

the Place of Poetry," where he explains the exile from reality which the artistic and the linguistic gesture compose, can Bonnefoy compare poetry with hope itself?[3] In the essay on Byzantium, he contrasts the remaining ruins to the former gold, the stone to the peacock's glory, associating the marks of the transitory with his own desire of "confronting the real in its most fugitive aspects, apparently those least charged with being, to consecrate them together with myself." (*R*, 10) In his essays and his poetry, the brilliant display of the peacock, classic symbol of luxurious profusion and aesthetic spectacle, clearly gives way to the more modest image of the stone (marking the limit between existence and nonexistence, the hardening of our human writing or *écriture*), to the fragment or the vestige (as opposed to the total and therefore abstract concept), and to the peacock's less spectacular substitute in this particular world of limited poetry, the salamander suddenly immobile on the wall. It is precisely this last image which forms the passage from the rejection of the static concept able only to dissociate the idea from the real (for instance, the fire, or the wall, or death) to the ensuing silence of the world about us and the perception now forced upon us of the "dreadful tautology of common speech." Finally, after the despair of this second period, we move to the optimistic recognition of a possible identification in poetic presence, where the specific image in its universal essence ("la salamandre") includes at once the salamander on this wall and all

---

[3] It is true that his terms are guarded ones: "Je *voudrais* réunir, je *voudrais* identifier *presque* la poésie et l'espoir" (italics mine).

others.[3a] This final experience of *order* is, for Bonnefoy, the practice of the sacred. ("French Poetry and the Principle of Identity," *R*)

"The word is the soul of what it names"; even if we do not create the world by naming it, we enter into it by that act, which is therefore not to be called futile. By naming we reassemble the real, whose "super-abundance" absorbs the poet and redeems him as well as his word. Bonnefoy's description of the poetic baptism of the salamander reveals in its mixture of metaphysical, religious, and concrete terms both his essential notion of place (*le lieu*) and of the poetic homage to reality, which, though its exterior elements will perish, is an interior and also sufficient ground for hope. "Let us say—for we must also save the word, and from its fatal desire to define everything—that its essence has spread out into the essence of other beings, like an analogical movement enabling me to perceive everything in the continuity and sufficiency of a *place*, and in the transparency of *unity*. The wall is justified, and the hearth, and the olive tree outside, and the earth." (*R*, 97) The miraculous appearance of the salamander on the wall now becomes the "unique angel" of poetry. The one appears in the place of the innumerable demons who have peopled the *mauvaise présence*, or the double against which the poetic presence struggles continually. In a final confidence, the poet is granted the

---

[3a] In *The Truth of Poetry* (London, Weidenfeld and Nicholson, 1969) Michael Hamburger claims that Bonnefoy's use here of the term "salamander" instead of "gecko" or "lizard" is a proof of the poet's subjectivity (pp. 241-43).

"great revelation of this eternal instant where all is given to me for me to understand and to link." (*R*, 98)

2. The Fragment and the Place

The humblest fragment of a wall and a torn bit of ivy leaf are instants of tangible presence in the face of intangible and stultifying concepts. Against the temptation of the static and perfect abstractions, they are the only possible salvation; this is also the theme of the brief poetic text beginning: "L'Imperfection est la cime." Imperfect as they are, they remain open to "what is":

But this broken leaf, greenish-black and dirtied, this leaf showing in its wound all the profundity of being, this infinite leaf is pure presence and consequently my salvation. Who could take away from me its having once been mine, and in a contact beyond destinies and locations, in the absolute? Who could destroy it, already destroyed?[4]

The theatre of potential poetic action is a tragic one because presence must soon change to absence, and the present immortality of which Bonnefoy speaks often bears the signature of the ephemeral by a sliding ("glissement") to the past tense of the verb. The traditionally abstract place of the universal becomes a *vrai lieu*, a true and specific place of conversion and cognizance, as concrete and significant as a statue, a combi-

[4] "Les Tombeaux de Ravenne," *L'Improbable* (Mercure de France, 1959), pp. 29-30.

nation of ancient oracle and actual homeland for the poet.[5]

Yet even here, in the *lieu-parole* where the word is completely identified with its situation, the truth of the word (*verité de parole*) cannot always be assured. All linguistic exercise entails for Bonnefoy a certain alienation from the essential: "Language is not the word. No matter how deformed or transformed our syntax, it will never be anything more than a metaphor of the impossible syntax, meaning nothing but exile." ("The Act and the Place of Poetry," *I*, 53) Language is not *logos*—it can serve to salute the procession of things passing, but it can neither become incarnate in these things, nor create them, nor endow them with eternal life. Nor should we expect the connection between perception and interior truth to be always apparent. Bonnefoy reminds us that while our words fascinate us they are robbing us of the real, for they cannot be the "real salvation." Language can retain nothing of the immediate, he says, referring to Hegel; the poem he mentions most often and in the most moving terms is Baudelaire's "À une passante." The act of speech may be no more than a pathetic gesture, no more forceful than any other activity in which we have not placed such hope. It is certainly no more essential than its situation, as for Bonnefoy a painting cannot be divorced from the place where we see it ("On Painting and Place," *R*) or a drama from its sacrificial surroundings.

[5] Elsewhere, Bonnefoy refers to Pompeii, a more startling example of life fixed in its attitudes as they become mere vestiges. Images of the immobile—photographs, murals, walls, stones— are the special signature of Bonnefoy's work.

To his notion of place Bonnefoy joins the notions of the true and the absolutely simple. After the most baroque ornamentation and the most frantic welcoming of all the manifestations of change, complicated forms will have consumed themselves to make way for a "second simplicity." He often uses the image of the *orangerie*, a place of the simplest structure and the greatest interior openness, where a necessary order banishes all the chaos of chance and of personality, revealing the *moi vacant* as it waits for "an intuition to fulfill it." This is the interior ideal, or the true place of the poetic theatre, not to be confused with the hothouses of other poetic attitudes. This structure is classic rather than exotic, universal rather than special, particular rather than symbolic, simple and sufficient rather than ornate. It represents the specific point of the universal: "Here (the true place is always a here), here mute or distant reality and my existence meet, are changed, exalted in the sufficiency of being." ("The Tombs of Ravenna," *I*, 23)[5a]

3. Finitude and Madness

A remarkable essay called "Baudelaire against Rubens" (1969) completes a trilogy of essential essays, of which "The Act and the Place of Poetry" of 1958, and "French Poetry and the Principle of Identity" of 1965 form the first two parts. It elaborates on the notion of salvation as the particular interiorization of the real, the rupture of the tragic individual from the mass of social beings involved only with surface "happiness," and the deliberate acceptance and absorption of death. It is in

[5a] See note 5a, added in proof, p. 170.

this sense also a continuation of two other essays, one on French gothic murals, where the arrested gestures of the subjects are made subordinate to the vitality and profusion of vegetation in its "deliberate shimmering presence," and another on the paintings of de Chirico, where the petrified objects force an awareness of the instant ("that place at that moment") in the very attempt to fix the atemporal, aggravating the sense of human finitude ("the western glory of an institution of death").

Only through a profound human pessimism is any real theory of poetry to be elaborated. For words and gestures, however poetic, remain divorced from their subject. The apparition we glimpse as eternal will once more fall into fragments and mere appearance. To Baudelaire's anguished questions: what can absolve us from this sin of writing? what is on the other side of it? Bonnefoy responds with his conviction on the place of poetry, that "it is the step left behind oneself, the track circling a great empty region, not to be entered but which is the place."[6] He replies further that the action of the work, limited as it is, is nevertheless sufficiently powerful to fascinate and to scandalize. We can therefore start from that point, seek at the very limits of sanity, "at the point where the poem breaks," rather than at the traditional place of unity, for the place of poetry. The value once attached to the notion of *symbol*, he says, is now attached to that of *symptom*. As the fragment is the truest representation of absolute pres-

[6] In *L'Ephémère*, no. 9, Spring 1969, p. 109. This journal's title proved appropriate; it has now ceased publication.

ence, so madness is the surest sign of "ouverture"—the only certain protection against the deadly equilibrium of an irremediable "clôture."[7]

4. THEATRE AND MYTH

Corresponding roughly to the three essays mentioned, Bonnefoy's three collections of poems can be taken as a tragic exposition of the theatre of dynamic and static alternations in the place as word, the *lieu-parole*: *Du Mouvement et de l'immobilité de Douve* (*Of the Motion and the Immobility of Douve*), 1953; *Hier régnant désert* (*Yesterday the Desert Reigning*), 1958; and *Pierre écrite* (*Written Stone*), 1965.[8] They replay essentially the same drama around the same few elements. It is played with the simplicity to which Bonnefoy so often pays homage ("The Second Simplicity," "Simple line," "Simple speech"), and yet the bare force of the understatement gives the drama all the ritual intensity of myth. The tension of verbal contrast leads from the initial presentation of spectacle ("je te voyais . . . je t'ai vue" . . . "je te vois"), by which the poet is separated from the actor, to the emotional assumption of the spectacle and gesture into the poet's voice (from "voir" to "voix"), and to the central series of debates between

---

[7] See remarks above on the desirable "faille" of the mute "e." Bonnefoy mentions also Baudelaire's use of the "cheville" as an attack on traditional closed prosody "par ces coups sourds contre la paroi de parole, par ce brisement de la perfection formelle et la catastrophe de la Beauté qu'il propose—en dépit de soi, on dépit de nous peut-être—à la poésie à venir . . ." ("L'Acte et le Lieu de la Poésie," I, p. 163).

[8] All published by Mercure de France. (*Du Mouvement et de l'immobilité de Douve, Hier régnant désert*, with 2 essays, coll. Poésie, Gallimard, 1970.)

149

speech and silence, the renascent phoenix and death, summer brightness and night, fire and wind, rupture and wholeness, presence and absence, between an opened and a closing path. In the final act, a sense of individual presence ("this tree") is perceived as one with the universal, in a place at once interior and exterior, where all elements reveal a unique coincidence of essence and existence: "true name," "true place," "true body."

As their names indicate, the three collections emphasize distinct perspectives on and moments of the drama. *Du Mouvement et de l'immobilité de Douve* presents the theatrical gesture, the poet's vision, the menace of final immobility, and the uncertainty as to whether it can be overcome. The book ends on a note of interrogation:

> Le jour franchit le soir, il gagnera
> Sur la nuit quotidienne.
> Ô notre force et notre gloire, pourrez-vous
> Trouer la muraille des morts? (p. 87)

> (Day crosses evening, catching up
> With daily night.
> Oh our strength and our glory, shall you
> Pierce the wall of the dead?)

Hier régnant désert poses against a series of voices a threat of silence in a place of sadness, against the possibility of movement, a threat of shipwreck and a dried-up path, and suggests the final acceptance of imperfection as the highest point of human drama:

Aimer la perfection parce qu'elle est le seuil,
Mais la nier sitôt connue, l'oublier morte,
L'imperfection est la cime. (p. 35)

(To love perfection as it is the threshold,
Denying it as soon as it is known, forgetting it once
 dead,
Imperfection is the summit.)

Pierre écrite opens with a ship's voyage in the motionless before revealing the poet's voice hardened into an
écriture and predicting the redemption of all things
human and changing by their participation in the un-
changing eternal:

À jamais le reflet d'une étoile immobile
Dans le geste mortel.

(Forever the reflection of a motionless star
In the mortal gesture.)

In the essay on Miró, the poet defines form as the
ordered structure man imposes on his expression and his
temporal shadow: "form is the *star* in him," linking each
being to the infinite unity. (*M*, 26) We might see Bonnefoy's recurring images—summer, star, ship, salamander, stone, birdsong—as this structure or the form
given to his own writing, the principle of its ordering.

The repetition of elements and themes is an essential
part of Bonnefoy's theory, as he states in the essay "La
Seconde simplicité"—moreover, the fragments of a
longer poem ("Dans le leurre du seuil," published in
L'Ephémère of autumn, 1969) take up once more the
themes of language—the appeal made to it, the pres-

ence or emptiness it solicits or betrays, or the "déchi-rure" and the nothingness felt in the poetic work—as well as the familiar images of reflection, fire, the ship, and the gesturing hand. The title is possibly an echo of the threshold of perfection tempting us to an immobile stance, which we must however overcome for a harder achievement of imperfection. Such poetic constancy is moving in its immobility. Nothing would be gained by separating the poet's work into stages or moments fur-ther than has already been indicated, since it is of a piece. A title toward the end of *Hier régnant désert* indicates an appropriate attitude: "La même voix, toujours."

Another echo of presence is found, appropriately, in the same place:

Ici, dans le lieu clair

. . .

Ici, et jusqu'au soir

. . .

Ici, toujours ici. (p. 72)

(Here, in the clear place

. . .

Here, and until the evening

. . .

Here, always here.)

And in *Pierre écrite,* a passage on the sufficiency of summer, on the poet's voyage through the seasons (where, in an effective telescoping of two uncompli-cated images, the means of travel is identified with the season, "navire d'un été") is paradoxical but persuasive, a perfect example of the intricate simplicity of all Bonnefoy's work:

Le mouvement
Nous était apparu la faute, et nous allions
Dans l'immobilité comme sous le navire
Bouge et ne bouge pas le feuillage des morts. (p. 13)

(Motion
Seemed error to us, and we moved
In immobility as under the ship
Moves and moves not the foliage of the dead.)

Throughout his texts, the poet is making an immobile pilgrimage toward unity and presence. ("Poetry and voyage are of the same stuff, of the same blood," says Bonnefoy after Baudelaire, calling them the only possible human actions "which have an end.")[9] The explicitly complicated attitude of remaining motionless while in motion is here seen as common to man and nature, a contradictory yet profoundly revealing gesture of the sort observed in all of Bonnefoy's writing. On the essential oppositions he builds an apparently fragile edifice of language, composed of brief poems with wide spaces, divisions into multiple parts, entitled or nontitled in purposely vague fashion—"A Voice Speaks," "A Stone," "True Place," "Place of the Salamander," "Place of the Deer."[10] But as the dramatic op-

[9] "Les Tombeaux de Ravenne" (i, p. 24).
[10] The deer is a traditional image associated with the figure of Christ in religious and metaphysical poetry—for instance, that of Jean de la Ceppède and Pierre-Jean Jouve. Bonnefoy's essay on the Gothic murals shows a fascination with the Room of the Deer in the Papal Palace.

positions are absorbed more and more into the texture of the poem itself—from the simple juxtaposition in the title "Du Mouvement et de l'immobilité de Douve" to the complex quotation above—the edifice proves itself of durable strength, and is in fact compared to a "written stone."

The stone chosen as the emblem of the poet signifies not just the acceptance of death or of the ruins of life, as has already been stated, but also the *borne* or marker placed at the limits of the path, the appropriate support for an *écriture* eternal in the instant, and the true and unadorned place where the poetic voice can be heard, the sacrificial scene of the doomed but infinitely significant gesture, and the bearer of the fatal message.[11]

5. POEM AND STONE

In the nineteen divisions of the poem "Théâtre," which introduces *Du Mouvement et de l'immobilité de Douve*, the poet-seer is immobile in the face of death. The repeated references to his attitude of onlooker are balanced with all the gestures of Douve dying but still active (running, raising her arm, lying down) which then slacken in pace until a series of verbs applied to her is suddenly passive in form: "couverte," "parcourue," "soumise," "écartelée," "parée," and her mouth, once open to cry out, is filled with earth, emptiness, and a ravine of cold. But she has exulted in the sensation of her own destruction (her head divided, her hands cloven), as it breaks the monotony of living; the repeated gesture of her raised arm, spotlighted, leads

[11] It is possibly also an allusion to the *Stèles* of Victor Ségalen.

directly to the apocalyptic vision of the village of em-
bers and the flames. In so far as she is the phoenix, the
verbs of rebirth, reassembling, and recapturing can be
applied to her, whereas the poet, able only to observe
the exaltation of the luminous dance ("je soutiens l'éclat
de tes gestes" / I sustain the brightness of your gestures), the lifted arm and the slowing down of the
gestures, has no other role to play than that of the
watcher ("le guetter," "le veilleur") waiting to observe
the rebirth in the landscape of ravine, forest, snow, and
wind.

Parallel to this initial duality is the immediately transferred or reversed energy of the cold "bleeding" on her
lips, chapped by the summer, and the windows white
from her blood. These may be read as the initial signs of
opposition then seen to be constants in all the poems:[12]
the word or the fire or the summer then silenced, extinguished, or chilled ("jour de parole . . . nuit de vent"/
day of word . . . night of wind), the vision reversed to
blindness, the action to effort lost, and the seizing already merged with the escaping: "Que saisir sinon qui
s'échappe?" (34) (What to seize if not the fleeing?)
Furthermore, the serious split between speech and gesture implies a certain distance from the word to the
world. The moments of optimism in the intensifying
power of poetry:

[12] As Jean Paris points out in his note "The New French
Poetry" (from *On Contemporary Literature*, ed. Kostelanetz,
Avon, 1964) the philosophic basis of Bonnefoy's poetry is Hege-
lian: every truth suppresses its opposite. The significance of
Douve lies in the awareness of death (which is life): it is, in
short, poetry confronting its own disappearance.

155

Douve, je parle en toi; et je t'enserre
Dans l'acte de connaître et de nommer (*D*, 45)

(Douve, I speak in you; and I enclose you
In the act of knowing and of naming)

Je ne suis que parole intentée à l'absence (*D*, 59)

(I am only speech held up against absence)

are challenged not simply by all the images of voices
extinguished, speech undone, lips blackened, birds fall-
en silent (as the phoenix may will itself forever dead)
but by a more terrible loss of faith in language:

Oui c'est bientôt périr de n'être que parole (*D*, 59)
(Yes, one perishes soon being no more than word)

Le peu de mots que nous fûmes (*PE*, 64)
(The few words we were)

The particular bitter self-consciousness haunting much
contemporary poetry is occasionally apparent here;
after a lyric passage, the poet remarks, "Ceci est une
image" (This is an image), and then points out that at
a certain depth images are no longer valid.

A solution will be found in *Pierre écrite*, however,
where the contemplation of a Tinteretto "Pietà" leads
suddenly to a perception of a necessary interrelation of
passion and language, language and life:

Le désir déchira le voile de l'image,
L'image donna vie à l'exsangue désir. (79)

(Desire rent the veil of the image,
The image gave life again to desire expiring.)

And in the brief poem on the power of poetry, the "Art de la poésie" which concludes *Pierre écrite*, the image desiccated and immobilized precedes the final redemption of the voice, as it is purified and saved, "lavée et rappelée." We can only assume from this that gesture ceases when the voice is to be redeemed. If we carry the assumption one step further, we see that it was necessary for the drama of Douve's immobilizing to be played out in order for the tombstone to be inscribed, the stone engraved, and the tablet traced, "pierre écrite" equalling in this sense "pierre tombale."

The reign of poetry in the present is the other and so far silent half of the phrase, "yesterday the desert reigned." Today poetry is at last supreme. As he waits in the barren landscape for the rebirth of the phoenix, the poet will hear a bird cry "like a sword." ("Le Chant de sauvegarde.") In the rock of the mountain a sign will be chiseled for him, signaling the end of his waiting and marking the beginning of a mythical task, linked by long tradition to the poetic tasks of heroes before him, as they drew the sword from the stone:

Ici dans l'herbe ancienne tu verras
Briller le glaive nu qu'il te faudra saisir. (56)

(Here in the old grass you will see
Shining the bare blade you must seize.)

Pain is implied within the action: this is "L'Ordalie," or the ordeal through which the hero must pass, the opposite pole from the *orangerie*, its calm double. (That this name should have been given also to a novel, although the latter was destroyed, indicates its importance;[12a] we might see it as related to the idea of threshold—*seuil*—and of *passage*.) As the image of blood is frequently associated with the voice, the path of poetic knowledge most frequently leads to the immobility of death:

> Des mots étaient gravés dans le sang de la pierre,
> Ils disaient le chemin de connaître et mourir. (59)

> (Words were incised in the blood of the stone,
> They told the path of knowing and dying.)

The poet's steps will be "de boue et nuit, de terre obscure" (of mud and night, of darkened earth); no flame is visible here, and finally there is no guide. The song of the bird is often menaced—like the bird, it plummets to earth, or it is stilled, or, again, it risks a dangerous journey and is shipwrecked. The poet's only passion, the song, has both saved him and lost him: "Le Chant de sauvegarde" ends with this final and most serious contradiction. Elsewhere, the repeated images such as the tree "lié et libre" (fettered and free) point to the necessary tension on which the poetry is centered. All the signs of voyage change to the negative or the closed form: "nul pas," "nul vaisseau," "nul cri," "fleuve nul," "chemins clos," "aile fermée." In a powerful group of poems called "Le Visage mort," the question is raised as to the success of the poetic journey which is the drama, whether the journey is seen as a pilgrimage by foot through forest and desert and mountain landscape, or by the traditional means of the ship, all images which

[12a] See note 12a, p. 170.

here meet in the ambiguous and extended ground of an interior poetry:

Le navire engagé dans l'angoisse des rives
Entrera-t-il enfin dans la salle du jour? (28)

(The ship engaged in the anguish of shores
Shall it come at last into the chamber of day?)

6. WOUND AND PATH

One of the odder and more significant characteristics of these texts is a particular, complex process of intensification. In the center of an element, the same element is repeated—or, conversely, from the center of an element, the essence of that element is projected. The exact opposite of the surrealist procedure for calling upon the marvelous, where one element is suddenly perceived in another ("l'un dans l'autre"), this sort of perception is a metaphysical one, linked at once to Bonnefoy's interpretation of the idea of repetition[13] and to his advocacy of the improbable. Contrary also to his theory of the positive negation—a perfectly understandable and genuinely valuable paradox, like his negative theologies—the attitude might be described as a double positive. It is an ultimate intricacy balancing an ultimate simplicity, and yet it appears in the guise of the simple. For instance, in a poem of an unelaborate title, "L'Arbre, La Lampe" (Tree, Lamp), the poet describes a tree

---

[13] Another of these examples could be taken from "Douve parle," the sequel to "Théâtre," but the image here carries a more traditional feeling; a voice speaking in the self now dead, laments: "Pourtant ce cri sur moi vient de moi/ Je suis muré dans mon extravagance." (*D*, 49)

growing old *within* the tree, and a bird going past the limit of birdsong (*PE*, 53), calling these qualities typical of the summer. In the long poem, "L'Eté de nuit," which introduces the collection, a poem which is in some senses a double of the "Théâtre" of the death of Douve,[14] the voyage made into immobility, into the

[14] Bonnefoy's great admiration for Baudelaire is based on his belief that the latter invented a certain idea of death as a fundamental aspect of the presence of things and of their reality. "Et Baudelaire va chercher à faire dire au poème cet extérieur absolu, ce grand vent aux vitres de la parole, *l'ici* et *le maintenant* qu'a sacralisés toute mort." (i, 162) This is the drama played out by the theatre of Douve, and the significance of her arrival at the place of the salamander; it is also another indication of the particular sense he attaches to the notion of the stone. His debate with Valéry ("Paul Valéry," i) turns about the same problem, couched in more romantic terms. Valéry has not known how to love things, says Bonnefoy, nor has he experienced that "essentielle joie mêlée de larmes qui arrache d'un coup l'oeuvre poétique à sa nuit." (144) He affirms, instead of the imperfection cherished by Bonnefoy (and Baudelaire, by implication), an art closed in form. "Dans une langue sans *e* muet—cette faille entre les concepts, cette intuition de la substance, cette chance extraordinaire du français—il identifie la forme à l'esprit qui oeuvre dans le conscience et le jour, sans avoir su qu'il n'y a de forme que pour la pierre, je veux dire pour la rupture et la nuit. Nous avons à oublier Valéry." (145) But he adds in a footnote that he is fighting against Valéry as one does against something in oneself.

For a superb example of concision and tragic poetic subtlety consult the recent edition of *Hier régnant désert* (following *Du Mouvement et de l'immobilité de Douve* in the collection Poésie, Gallimard, 1970), where the four poems of "le Feuillage éclairé" (pages 51 to 54 of the 1958 edition of *Hier régnant désert*) are combined into one brief and far more effective one. Each change is significant.

A. First, of the two initial verses in the original poem, the latter one is eliminated, leaving only the one verse sharply isolated from the remainder of the text as a striking prefatory question: "Dis-tu qu'il se tenait sur l'autre rive?" Then, underlining

garden and the river, reveals a division and doubling of perception: "Et le feuillage aussi brille sous le feuillage" (*PE*, 11) (And the foliage too shines beneath the foliage). There is a greater number of these suggestions of what we might term an *interior infinite* in *Pierre*

the brevity and solemnity of that beginning, the next two lines which had been of approximately the same length, standing thus in a balance with the first two verses, are now transformed by one simple suppression of adverbial phrase into an unequal pair, the first by its fragmentary nature pointing back to the gap in the text after the question. Compare the two versions:

1. Dis-tu qu'il se tenait sur l'autre rive,
   Dis-tu qu'il te guettait à la fin du jour?
   L'oiseau dans l'arbre de silence avait saisi
   De son chant vaste et simple et avide nos coeurs . . .

2. Dis-tu qu'il se tenait sur l'autre rive?
   L'oiseau avait saisi
   De son chant vaste et simple et avide nos coeurs. . . .

B. Then, the second and the fourth of the original sections of the poem, formally the weakest, are eliminated, and the second stanza of the third is added to the now altered first part, to which it forms a perfect conclusion, night responding to night, the image of the torn robe responding to the rupture or tear in the text visually marked by the dots of omission:

> . . . L'Ange de vivre ici, le tard venu
> Se déchirait comme une robe dans les arbres.

In a letter to the author (June 4, 1971), Bonnefoy writes: "Tout de même, j'attache beaucoup d'importance aux points de suspension."

C. In the original description of language as it moves in the landscape of loss:

> Avec le mouvement des mots dans les ramures
> Pour appeler encore, pour aimer vainement
> Tout ce qui est perdu,

the branches are changed to leaves, "parmi les feuilles," so that the final "feuillage" marking the angel's motion now corresponds to those "feuilles" of the human movement:

écrite than in the first two collections, and a greater subtlety of means by which the same drama is replayed. A text labeled simply "Une Pierre" begins: "Le jour au fond du jour . . ." (*PE*, 64) (Day at the depth of day . . .). The original perception opens out on the inside in a deliberate creation of profundity, a sort of *mise-en-abyme* of contemplation.

"The image must be annulled by the image for the invisible to be felt." This sentence from the essay "French Poetry and the Principle of Identity" and a one-sentence paragraph from Bonnefoy's essay on the painter Balthus are perhaps the best definitions of the poet's starting-point in the complex for his voyage to the simple. Discussing the melancholy pride of that painter, his energy constantly at war with the obstacles of emptiness and boredom in order to provoke a state of psycho-

---

Ses jambes de feuillage sous les lampes
Paraissaient par matière et mouvement et nuit.

The foliage is then illuminated, as in the title of the poem, by the words of men and by the miraculous presence of the moment, in this *place*.

D. And finally a detail of intensification: the comma after the loss in the first version "tout ce qui est perdu" is changed to a full stop. For the place and moment to be seen in their full significance, they must include the absolute certainty of temporal disappearance and the absolute vanity of human love and language.

And, in the general rearrangement of the poems, several series of themes are reinforced—those of fire, of infinity, of eternity. A far more positive feeling is conveyed. But Bonnefoy sees his second text in no way as a correction of the first, rather as his rereading of it in 1970. The two texts then stand as parallel possibilities for our contemplation, and for his. The poet here relegates his traditionally privileged role in order to become the reader of the poem. (In a conversation with the author.)

logical unrest, Bonnefoy remarks: "But that is the necessary danger, the negation on which everything can
be based." To define French poetry, Bonnefoy uses the
term *contre-jour*, the light found in the darkest places,
which rarely changes to the light of noon. He locates
his poetry in what he calls the other and warmer *contre-
jour*,[15] in the light of evening. ("French Poetry," *R*, 124)
Thus, the danger of immobility creates for him the only
sufficiently interesting mobility, imperfection is the real
summit of human experience, and it is only the threat
of silence which confers value on the word. His most
remarkable essays are called, with every reason,
L'Improbable; he dedicates them to:

> . . . the improbable, that is to say what is.
> To a spirit of watchfulness. To negative theologies.
> To a poetry desired, a poetry of rains, of waiting and
> of wind.
> To a great realism which complicates rather than
> resolving,
> which points out the obscure, which holds clarity
> to be clouds
> that can always be torn apart. Which concerns
> itself with a
> high and pathless clarity. (*I*, 7)

What is most probable is not only least real for the poet,
but least satisfactory as grounds for the poetic, defined
in this case as an intensity based on conflict. So, in

[15] Compare with the technique of *counter-light* portraits; a
great many of Bonnefoy's poems and utterances show the subtle-
ties of that particular contrast.

"Douve parle," the voice speaking counsels the least obvious path: in order for the night to be at its extreme point of elevation, "plus haute," and for the dawn to bring only the wind of sterility, one must plead for the self's blindness, its destruction, and its silence:

> Demande pour tes yeux que les rompe la nuit
>
> . . .
>
> Demande pour ta voix que l'étouffe la nuit (58)
>
> (For your eyes, ask that the night shatter them
>
> . . .
>
> For your voice, ask that the night stifle it)

The explanation given for the desire of destruction is the construction of a more permanent strength after the consuming of the charred remains:

> Tant de chemins noircis feront bien un royaume
> Où rétablir l'orgueil que nous avons été
> Car rien ne peut grandir une éternelle force
> Qu'une éternelle flamme et tout soit défait. (57)
>
> (So many blackened paths will surely make a
>   kingdom
> Where we may rebuild the pride we used to be,
> For nothing can strengthen an eternal might
> But an eternal flame and a total undoing.)

And again, in *Hier régnant désert*, the poet emphasizes the sacrificial gesture as the only possible poetic entry to what is beyond beauty and form:

> Il y avait qu'il fallait détruire et détruire et détruire,
> Il y avait que le salut n'est qu'à ce prix.

Ruiner la face nue qui monte dans le marbre,
Marteler toute forme toute beauté. (35)

(One had to destroy and destroy and destroy
Salvation was at that price alone.
Ruining the bare face arising in the marble,
Striking all forms all beauty.)

In almost every series of poems, the image of the wound plays a dominant role. In *Du Mouvement* . . . , a secret rupture is revealed, the poem tears apart, and the water makes a wound in the stones of day. In the last volume, the shoulder of the sky is torn, and finally the stones are unsealed. All of these images merge into the one truth of the word, the *verité de parole* which we might here call the truth of the image: for the stone to be deciphered, for the world to be opened to the comprehension of the poet ("le rayonnement de pierres descellées"/ the radiance of stones unsealed),[16] a preliminary suffering is inevitable. Douve is the name of a depression in the stones:

Douve profonde et noire,
Eau basse irréductible où l'effort se perdra. (76)

(Douve deep and dark,
Low-lying water irreducible where all effort will
be lost.)

At the conclusion of the "Théâtre" of which she is the heroine, her smile is seen as an "ouverture tentée dans l'épaisseur du monde" (29) (an opening tried in the

---

[16] So the alchemists' "real gold" or light of knowledge is only attained by uncovering the philosophers' stone.

density of the world). The key words of this theatre: "Douve," "ouverture," "où mourir," "jour," all have this break in them,[17] the depression or the circular depth (*ou*) of sound enabling them to be the carriers of the suffering, each becoming "cette pierre ouverte," this stone split open, which is the sacrificial path. As the name Douve leads into the "ouverture tentée," the wound signals the way which is finally to be that of the real presence; the elevation of total emptiness, "ce vide où je te hausse," prefigures the time of fullness. The question as to the success of the pilgrimage is now answered.

In *L'Ordalie*, after the testing, after an initial and serious doubt as to the possible entry of being into the world of the word, the response is positive:

Mais enfin le feu se leva,
Le plus violent navire
Entra au port. (*H*, 34)

(But finally the fire arose,
The most violent ship
Entered the port.)

[17] Michel Deguy describes, in "La Poésie en question" (*Modern Language Notes*, May, 1970), the intimate relation of the poet to the idea of rupture: he relies on the break or division between two elements or on their meeting: "une charnière (pli, jointure, feuillure, brisure)" in order to separate the notions of here and there. For another example of the confrontation with rupture, see Maurice Blanchot's statement of literary purpose (*La Part du feu*, Gallimard, 1949, p. 306): "Faire en sorte que la littérature devint la mise à découvert de ce dedans vide, que tout entière elle s'ouvrit à sa part de néant, qu'elle réalisât sa propre irréalité. . . ." See also Philippe Sollers, *Logiques*, 9-10, 12, and *passim*, on the *texts of rupture*.

7. PICTURE

The desert has yielded to the garden of the one sala-mander ("Lieu de la salamandre") and the one tree, where the moment replaces the abstraction of tradi-tional concepts and the painful gestures of ritual drama. The poet and the reader are illuminated by "un éblouis-sement dans les mots anciens" (75) (a radiance in the ancient words). Most significant, the past is supplanted by the actual, yesterday ("hier") by what is present ("ici"), the myth by the acknowledgment of what is now possible:[17a]

> . . . Les fruits anciens
> Soient notre faim et notre soif enfin calmées.
> Le feu soit notre feu. Et l'attente se change
> En ce proche destin, cette heure, ce séjour. (78)

> (. . . The ancient fruits
> May they be our hunger and our thirst appeased at
>   last.
> May the fire be our fire. And may the waiting be
>   changed
> To this near fate, this hour, this place.)

In a brief passage called "Le Livre, pour vieillir" a great silence comes from the book to the heart, signal-ing the end of dramatic action, the beginning of con-templation. Time ceases, and the present is seen as sufficient:

> Simples dans le verger sont les fruits mûrs (69)

> (Simple in the orchard are the ripe fruits)

[17a] See note 17a, p. 170.

In the specific motionless moment no future is predicted. Nothing formerly important is any longer taken seriously. The fruits are already ripened; the poet questions even the necessity of the voyage he has made:

Et je m'étonne alors qu'il ait fallu
Ce temps, et cette peine. Car les fruits
Régnaient déjà dans l'aube. Et le soleil
Illuminait déjà le pays du soir (73)

(And I am astonished then that it took
This time, and this pain. For the fruits
Reigned already in the dawn. And the sun
Lit already the landscape of evening)

The spaciousness created within the verse by the central pause denies in its tranquility the possible active opposition of the title: "Le Dialogue d'angoisse et de désir." No room remains for future gesture: no appeal will be made outside the border of this place. The *orangerie* is absorbed into the stone.[17b] The poet speaks of immobility, which is not to say that he is speaking of death: "Oui, je puis vivre ici. . . ." (80) (Yes, I can live here . . .).

The place of conversion, one of the formulas Bonnefoy applies to his notion of the true place, is here a persuasion to inscribe forever all actions within a *chosen fixity*, an invitation

À de grands chemins clos, ou venait boire l'astre
Immobile d'aimer, de prendre, et de mourir (*PE*, 61)

(To great closed paths, where the motionless star
Of living, of taking, and of dying came to drink)

[17b] See note 17b, p. 170.

The eternal reflection of an immobile star always present in human gesture has now redeemed that gesture. Time loses its force, as all movement turns into mere painting, frozen for our unhurried and motionless aesthetic enjoyment.[18] It is precisely in "La Lumière du soir," that ambiguous *contre-jour* of evening light which perfectly situates the poetry of the interior infinite, that the most innocent and portentous statement of the halted universe appears:

Et le temps reste autour de nous comme des flaques de couleur. (*PE*, 59)

(And time remains around us like pools of color.)

What is this if not a spectacle, at least as *picturesque* as it is poetic? In the ambiguous pilgrimage toward presence, all movement perceived outwardly and intuited inwardly comes to an apparent halt in the here and the now. The serious wager Bonnefoy takes up against the Valéry of a perfect or closed poetry, the private battle which fascinates him because it must be fought within himself, is not acted out for our benefit as spectators. The Theatre once played in front of us as well as of the poet observing has now moved to a more

---

[18] But here again, there may be more movement in painting than it would appear from its contrast with cinema. Ernest Gombrich (*Art and Illusion*, Bollingen, Princeton, 1969; from Mellon Lectures, 1956), observes that once we become aware of the motion in a painting, the ground against which we see it becomes a *screen* upon which it takes place, as if it were indeed cinematic action. Compare the point of view of Charles Lapicque (*Essais sur l'espace, l'art et la destinée*, Grasset 1958), where the motion of the spectator seeing the immobile canvas is associated with that in the painting (p. 194).

secret scene within the true place of our joined imagina-
tions. Only the *actors* are permitted in the true place of
poetic adventure, where they alone can distinguish between motion and immobility.

[5a] "Et moi, soucieux d'une transcendance mais aussi d'un lieu
où elle aurait sa racine. . . ." (*L'Arrière-Pays*, Skira, 1972, p. 45)

[12a] Another work, with an equally significant title, was also
destroyed to prevent any possible *closure* of experience: "Je
déchirai *Le Voyageur* parce que je ne voulais pas l'écriture imaginative, et scellée, mais l'analyse avertie, condition de l'expérience
morale." (*L'Arrière-Pays*, p. 100)

[17a] And in the later *L'Arrière-Pays*, "La terre *est*, le mot *présence* a un sens." (p. 149) Of this country at once removed and
present, the poet says: "Personne n'y marcherait comme sur
terre étrangère." (p. 7)

[17b] Here the word, never part of a "texte clos," is opened by
the vision: "Ce sera lui le creuset où l'arrière-pays s'étant dissipé,
se reforme, où l'ici vacant cristallise. Et où, quelques mots pour
finir brilleront peut-être, qui, bien que simples et transparents,
comme le rien du langage, seront pourtant tout, et réels."
(*L' Arrière-Pays*, p. 149)

5 FIVE

CONCLUSION

The Moment and the Page—
Scene of the Double Spectacle

AGAIN we turn to Bonnefoy's celebration of the *written stone* doubling the page and to the tombstone inscribed, both testimonials to the permanence and the serious art of the game. In the parable called a poem, *l'Anti-Platon*, a man engraves messages on three playing cards—for these also are our pages. Here we read the following inscriptions: "Eternité, je te hais!" "Que cet instant me délivre!" "Indispensable mort." (Eternity, I hate you! Let this instant deliver me! Indispensable death.) From Plato's cave to the noisy room where this man is imprisoned the distance is immeasurable. It is not absolute Ideas or ideals of perfection which count for Bonnefoy or for any of the poets discussed here, but rather the present moment, the objects it carries within it, and its passing. To sit shuffling the cards with their mortal *écriture* (as far from the tablets of

Moses as from the Platonic Ideas) is at the same time
to make a deliberate gesture toward a human destiny,
a gesture perhaps melodramatic, certainly imperfect,
but the only one possible in these circumstances:

> Ainsi sur la faille du temps marche-t-il, éclairé par
> sa blessure.

> (So over the fault of time he walks, illumined
> by his wound.)

To make of this *fault*, then, our illumination: only a poet
would be guided by that resolve.

The only place we have is determined by the spectacle given us; the page is finally our screen and our circus
ring, our playing board, scene, and canvas. Whether it
is to become the "vrai lieu," the actual location of poetry and of theatre, depends on the intensity of our gaze
and the force of our language. The possibility of a present epic resides in our giving to the playing cards, by
whatever name we choose to call them, a sufficient order, weight, and significance of inscription, so that they
may become our "pierres écrites." Artaud's meditation
on one hair is, in this setting, of no less value than
Tzara's circus, Cendrars' cinema, or Bonnefoy's canvas.
All the explosiveness of language sought after and
achieved by Péret and the other surrealists in the great
game of poetry can be brought to bear on whatever we
may have about us as stage props, to function in whatever frame we choose or are granted. When Bonnefoy
begins his poem against Plato and in praise of the moment, we may take that moment also as a text where

the *gesture* must be made and seen in the light of its necessary fault which redeems it:

Il s'agit bien de *cet* objet. . . . (9)

(It is really a question of *this* thing. . . .)

And it is still the gesture that matters, visible or not, definable or not. Let its trace be classified as cinematic, poetic, linguistic, theatrical, or aesthetic: the category has no effect on its potential force. The marvelous implied in the mere possibility of movement, the unique passion of setting in motion, the certain value of a motion made and conferred by its making, these dominate the tragedy of the motion stopped, of the canvas fixed on the wall, of the film, the circus, and the game ended.

Of course these essays have their end too; at a given point, the motion through the series of meditations on motion ceases. Does the end of movement contained within every movement invalidate its spectacle or its significance, does the sense of passing invalidate the scene of passage? All we are sure of is that the play is restricted in some fashion by the page, that the theatre beyond the text depends on the matter given in the text, and on nothing else.

From Tzara's "Note on poetry" and his "Note on art" with their praise of the unmediated clarity of the quickest gesture to Artaud's *Théâtre et son double* as an always-present concern with the doubled tragic ritual of representation, from Péret's *Grand jeu* and his confidence in the language of daybreak to Crevel's suicide and the haunting surrealist images of mirrors and shipwreck, and from Cendrars' eulogy of the present,

173

from his *Profond aujourd'hui* to Bonnefoy's *Hier ré-gnant désert* as a nostalgic intrusion of yesterday's im-perfection and the prediction of permanence ("pierres à venir"/ stones yet to come) into the perfect and un-moving instant of the actual place, the distance in time, location, and language is evident enough. It stretches from a rapid-action cinema and circus through the ritual transaction of game and the slower-paced symbolism of theatre to take its final position in, or rather on the other side of, the immobility of the painted image.

The specific poetic gesture of each of these writers has its own location in that trajectory, its own appro-priate scene and theatre props, its own space, deter-mined by its chosen rhythm. But on occasion the theat-rical space of one overlaps with the space of another, and the gestures for a moment coincide, as is to be ex-pected in a text touching on simultaneity and futurism, on the techniques of ideograph and montage. So Cen-drars' poem on the Medrano circus stands beside Tzara's salute to the circus performer, and to the ringmaster— that is, to himself as acrobat of poetry and choreog-rapher of the poetic dance, while Cendrars' essays on the cinema inhabit the same space as those of Artaud and the other surrealists. Artaud's *théâtre par la poésie*, or theatre by means of poetry, can be seen, if we care to see it so, as part of the same series with the nineteen poems of Bonnefoy's "Théâtre" telling of the death of Douve, or Artaud's anguished reflections on myth and ritual as part of the series including Bonnefoy's poems of sword and rock with their legendary Arthurian tone and matter, of birdsong, salvation, and silence.

Bonnefoy's allusions to shipwreck take a great part of their strength from the poetic accumulation around that image. Similarly, his use of the stone as support for the *trace* of writing is all the more impressive for its poetic transformation of the Mallarméan image of the white page; his meditations on the special significance of the deer's movements among the foliage acquire depth and resonance from their echoing of the imagery so often used by Jean de la Ceppède and Pierre-Jean Jouve. The contribution of present context is reinforced by the accumulated weight of past literary experience, the place of a particular theatre enlarged and the intensity of the theatrical gesture sharpened by a consciousness of the space beyond the theatre which is finally, by the implications of the reader's own gesture of reading, included in the true scene of poetry. For the *apparent* gesture of the text must be finally treated as the road to an *inner* gesture, to the real place of poetry and the poetic word. The only privileged entry to this inner theatre of poetry is that of the actor as he is defined here, a personage projected from the space of the text, created by the look exchanged between the reader and author in the moment of the reading.

"We must realize the possibility of text as theatre as well as of the theatre and life as a text if we want to take up our position in the writing which defines us," explains Philippe Sollers in his *Logiques*.[1] From the text and the reader's participation in it comes a double illumination, playing over the surface—but of the moving or the frozen gesture of the entire inner space, even

---

[1] Philippe Sollers, *Logiques* (Seuil, 1968).

the actor is never sure. Thus the implied doubt of necessity in the poetic scene and in the doubled theatre of the textual gesture, which perfectly responds to, or corresponds to, the initial doubling of personality and play.

"Je suis tel que je me suis vu" (I am as I have seen myself to be).[2] Thus Artaud formulates the basic perception linking rôle to reality. The act of observing places the spectator already at a distance from the personality observed, even if it is his own. And yet that distance, that split in being, functions not only as a source for the consciousness obsessed with doubling and otherness (the sickness of the divided self, the violently impoverished or stolen spirit, the powerlessness of language) but also as the source for renascent personality. Impotence is suddenly made the ground of act: the role becomes the actor's identification, his true being, by an effort of will. The speaker occupies the present ("Je suis"), identifying himself with his appearance ("tel que . . .") while actor and spectator are relegated to the past ("Je me suis vu"), so that in the space of this single sentence, a drama of action and vision, of being and time plays itself out, compressing motion into a brief linguistic unity.

[2] Artaud continues his description of the doubling of personality into actor and creator and of its advantages over the single, one-perspective state: "Je suis tantôt dans la vie tantôt au-dessus de la vie. Je suis comme un personnage de théâtre qui aurait le pouvoir de se considérer lui-même, et d'être tantôt abstraction, pure et simple création de l'esprit, et tantôt inventeur et animateur de cette créature d'esprit. Il aurait alors tout en vivant la faculté de nier son existence et de se dérober à la pression de son antagoniste qui, lui demeurerait lui-même, d'un bout à l'autre, et d'un seul bloc, vu toujours par le même côté."

If we keep in mind Artaud's meditation on the double *act* as well as on the single line, if we recognize the many sets of dual images haunting contemporary theory, all the double mirrors and communicating vessels essential to the thought of our poets,[3] we should not wonder that the figures of poetic language itself are double, that the linguistic theatre shows an exterior and dramatic face to us as long as we are willing to look only at that face, observing the appearance of motion, as well as another interior face which can be contemplated only by the participating actor who is properly at home in a scene inside the text, in a passage beyond the traditional place of play. Here the reiterations of a single gesture or word, the recurring visions of a few images larger than life (such as Bonnefoy's salamander, or deer, or the river and the orangery around which his poems turn) might seem no longer the tranquil witnesses to a continuing drama reassuring to us as critics since we can observe them, speaking of their reappearance and of their importance. They might, if only we could see them in their proper and interior lighting, be revealed to us as the terrible, because instantly exhausted, moments of salvation for the poet, and for the actor in whose performance we have a part.

In the game of the inner theatre as it is played out in poetry, we may have to start out again—as did the surrealist poets—with our eyes willingly closed to the logical impossibilities of the double gesture, of the static

[3] Poetry, that is, taken in the broadest sense, and represented, just among the Dada and surrealist groups, by such different figures as Aragon, Breton, Duprey, Eluard, and Rigaut.

mobility and the mobile arrest, of what Tzara calls the clear darkness of Dada: "Obscurity is creative if it is such a bright and pure illumination that our fellow men are blinded by it."[4] In any contemporary poetic situation, we acknowledge the presence of a double spectacle, accepting that spectacle as the true place of theatre in poetry, the genuine mark of poetic language, forever distinguished in its ambiguous gesture from ordinary discourse as it moves across a single scene.

[4] Tristan Tzara, *Sept manifestes Dada, suivis de Lampisteries,* p. 107.

WORKS REFERRED TO
OR CONSULTED

(Unless otherwise stated, the place of publication is Paris
for books in French, and New York for those in English.)

Louis Aragon, *Le Mouvement perpétuel*. Gallimard, 1926.
 Le Paysan de Paris. Gallimard, 1926.
 Une Vague de rêves. Privately printed, 1924.
Antonin Artaud, *Oeuvres*, 1961- , particularly volumes I
 ("L'Art et la Mort," "Le Pèse-Nerfs," "L'Ombilic des
 Limbes," "Bilboquet"); III ("A Propos du cinéma"); IV
 ("Le Théâtre et son Double"); and VII ("Au Pays des
 Tarahumaras").
Yves Bonnefoy, *Anti-Platon* (avec *Le Coeur-espace*), Gale-
 rie Maeght, 1962.
  Préface a Léon Chestov, *Oeuvres*, volume 3 (*Athènes
  et Jérusalem*), Flammarion, 1967.
  Léonor Fini ou la profondeur délivrée. Galerie Iolas,
  1965.
  Hier régnant désert. Mercure de France, 1958.
  L'Improbable. Mercure de France, 1959.
  Miró. Milan, Silvana, 1964.
  Du Mouvement et de l'immobilité de Douve. Mercure
  de France, 1953. Reprinted with *Hier régnant désert*,
  Anti-Platon, and two essays. Gallimard, 1970.
  Peintures murales de la France gothique. Hartmann,
  1954.

Pierre écrite. Mercure de France, 1965.

Un Rêve fait à Mantoue. Mercure de France, 1967. Includes *La Seconde simplicité*, essays on Byzantium, Giacometti, etc.

Rome, 1630: L'Horizon du premier baroque. Coll. Les Balances du temps, Flammarion, 1970.

L'Arrière-Pays. Coll. Les Sentiers de la création, Skira, 1972.

André Breton, *Poèmes.* Gallimard, 1948; reprinted 1953.

Guy Cabanel, *Maliduse.* St.-Lizier, privately printed, 1961.

Blaise Cendrars, *Aujourd'hui.* Grasset, 1931. Includes "Profond Aujourd'hui," "J'ai tué," "L'ABC du cinéma," etc.

Blaise Cendrars: 1887-1961. Mercure de France, 1962.

Blaise Cendrars vous parle. Denoël, 1952.

Dites-nous, Monsieur Blaise Cendrars. Lausanne, Editions Rencontre, 1969.

La Fin du monde filmée par l'ange Notre Dame. Seghers, 1949.

Histoires vraies. Grasset, 1938.

Hommage à Blaise Cendrars (Institut français de Modène). Rome, Editions Lucca, 1961.

Inédits secrets (présentation par Miriam Cendrars). Club français du livre, 1969.

Le Lotissement du ciel. Denoël, 1949.

Joseph Lovey, *Situation de Blaise Cendrars.* Neuchatel, A la Baconnière, 1965.

Du Monde entier, Poésies complètes: 1912-1914.

Au Coeur du monde, Poésies complètes: 1924-1929. Gallimard, 1967 (collection Poésie).

Oeuvres complètes, volume I. Club français du livre.

Selected Writings of Blaise Cendrars. (Ed. and tr. Walter Albert), New Directions, 1962; reprinted 1966.

Trop c'est trop. Denoël, 1957.

Vol à voile. Lausanne, La Petite Ourse, 1931.

René Crevel, *Êtes-vous fous?* Gallimard, 1929; reprinted, 1969.

Robert Desnos, *Cinéma.* Gallimard, 1966.
Domaine public. Gallimard, 1953.
La Liberté ou l'amour! Kra, 1927; reprinted, Gallimard, 1962.

Benjamin Péret, *Anthologie de l'amour sublime.* Albin Michel, 1956.
Anthologie des mythes, légendes et contes populaires d'Amerique. Albin Michel, 1960.
Benjamin Péret. Seghers, 1961 (collection Poètes d'aujourd'hui).
Le Grand jeu. Gallimard, 1928; reprinted in volume i of Péret, *Oeuvres,* Losfeld, 1969.
Le Livre de Chilam Balam de Chumayel, Denoël, 1955.
Je sublime, Ed. Surréalistes, 1936; reprinted in *Feu central,* K. éditeur, 1947.
Péret's Score. (Ed. and tr. J. H. Matthews), Minard, 1965.

Tristan Tzara, *L'Arbre des Voyageurs.* (Includes "L'Arbre des Voyageurs," "À Perte de Nuages," "Le Feu defendu.") Editions de la Montagne, 1930.
L'Homme approximatif. Editions de la Fourcade, 1931 (reprinted, Gallimard, 1968, collection Poésie).
Approximate Man and Other Writings. (Translated, with introduction and notes, by Mary Ann Caws), Detroit, Wayne State University Press, 1972.
Midis gagnés. (Includes "Abrégé de la nuit," "La Main passe," "Les Mutations radieuses," "Midis gagnés.") Denoël, 1939.
Morceaux choisis. Bordas, 1947.
Les Mutations radieuses (in *Midis gagnés*).
De nos oiseaux. Kra, 1923.
Les Premiers poèmes. Seghers, 1965.

Works Referred to or Consulted

Sept manifestes dada, suivis de lampisteries. Pauvert, 1963.

Vingt-cinq poèmes dada. Zurich, Collection Dada, 1918.

Vingt-cinq et un poèmes. Fontaine, 1946.

JOURNALS:

Archibras
La Brêche, action surréaliste
Communications
Coupure
Dyn
L'Ephémère
Médium
Minotaure
Mouvement
Yale French Studies (Surrealism Issue).

ANTHOLOGIES:

Jean-Louis Bédouin, *La Poésie surréaliste.* Seghers, 1964.

Serge Gavronsky, *Poems and Texts.* October House, 1969.

J. H. Matthews, *An Anthology of French Surrealist Poetry.* Minneapolis, 1966.

SOME CRITICAL WORKS:

Ferdinand Alquié, ed. *Le Surréalisme* (Entretiens de la décade surréaliste, Cerisy-la-Salle), Mouton, 1968.

Anna Balakian, *Surrealism: The Road to the Absolute.* Noonday Press, 1959; Random House, 1970.

Mary Ann Caws, *The Poetry of Dada and Surrealism: Aragon, Breton, Tzara, Eluard, Desnos.* Princeton, Princeton University Press, 1970.

Claude Courtot, *Introduction à la lecture de Benjamin Péret.* Le Terrain Vague, 1965.

Herbert Gershman, *The Surrealist Revolution in France.* Ann Arbor, The University of Michigan Press, 1969.

Naomi Greene, *Antonin Artaud: Poet Without Words.* Simon and Schuster, 1970.

Manuel L. Grossman, *Dada: Paradox, Mystification, and Ambiguity in European Literature.* Pegasus, 1971.

Bettina L. Knapp, *Antonin Artaud: Man of Vision.* David Lewis, 1969; Avon (Discus Books), 1971.

J. H. Matthews, *Surrealist Poetry in France.* Syracuse, Syracuse University Press, 1969.

Elmer Peterson, *Tristan Tzara.* New Brunswick, N.J., Rutgers University Press, 1970.

Michel Sanouillet, *Dada à Paris.* Pauvert, 1966.

Eric Sellin, *The Dramatic Concepts of Antonin Artaud.* Chicago and London, The University of Chicago Press, 1968.

WORKS CONSULTED:

Guillaume Apollinaire, *Chroniques d'art* (1902-1918), ed. L. C. Breunig, Gallimard, 1960.
> *Les Peintres cubistes,* ed. L. C. Breunig and J.-Cl. Chevalier, coll. Miroirs de l'art, Hermann, 1965.

Rudolf Arnheim, *Art and Visual Perception: A Psychology of the Creative Eye.* Berkeley, University of California Press, 1956 (fourth reprinting, 1969).
> *Film.* London, Faber and Faber, 1933.
> *Visual Thinking.* Berkeley, 1969.

Owen Barfield, *Poetic Diction: A Study in Meaning.* London, Faber and Faber, 1927; McGraw-Hill, 1964.

Pär Bergman, *"Modernolatria" et "Simultanéità": Recherches sur deux tendances dans l'avant-garde littéraire en Italie et en France à la veille de la première guerre mondiale,* Studia litterarum Upsaliensa 11, Svenska Bokforlaget/ Bonniers, Uppsala, 1962.

Maurice Blanchot, *L'Entretien infini.* Gallimard, 1969.
> *La Part du feu.* Gallimard, 1949.

Works Referred to or Consulted

Kenneth Burke, *Language as Symbolic Action: Essays on Life, Literature, and Method.* Berkeley, University of California Press, 1966.
> *The Philosophy of Literary Form: Studies in Symbolic Action.* Vintage, 1957.

Michel Butor, *Répertoire II* and *III.* Gallimard, 1964, 1968.

Francis Carmody, *Cubist Poetry: The School of Apollinaire.* Berkeley (no publisher listed), 1954.

Douglas Cooper, *The Cubist Epoch,* Los Angeles County Museum of Art and The Metropolitan Museum of Art, 1971.

Robert Delaunay, *Du Cubisme à l'art abstrait,* documents inédits publiés par Pierre Francastel, S.E.V.P.E.N., 1957.

Jacques Derrida, *L'Ecriture et la différence.* Seuil, 1967.
> *De la Grammatologie.* Ed. Minuit, 1967.

Sergei Eisenstein, *Film Essays and a Lecture.* New York and Washington, Praeger, 1970.
> *The Film Form* (tr. Jay Leyda). Harcourt, Brace, 1949.
> *The Film Sense* (tr. Jay Leyda). Harcourt, Brace, 1942.

Michel Foucault, *Les Mots et les Choses.* Gallimard, 1966.

Pierre Francastel, *Peinture et Société: Naissance et destruction d'un espace plastique de la Renaissance au Cubisme.* Lyon, Audin, 1951.

Joseph Frank, *The Widening Gyre: Crisis and Mastery in Modern Literature.* New Brunswick, N.J., Rutgers University Press, 1963.

Pierre Garnier, *Spatialisme et poésie concrète.* Gallimard, 1968.

Jacques Garelli, *La Gravitation poétique.* Mercure de France, 1966.

Ernest Gombrich, *Art and Illusion.* Princeton, Princeton University Press, 1960 (first paper edn., reprinted 1969).

Ian Graham, *The Art of Maya Hieroglyphic Writing,* Cambridge, Harvard University Press, 1971 (Catalogue of Exhibition at the Peabody Museum).

Robert Graves, *Poetic Craft and Principle*. London, Cassell, 1967.

Harvey Gross, ed., *The Structure of Verse: Modern Essays on Prosody*. Fawcett, 1966.

Irving Howe, ed., *Literary Modernism*. Fawcett, 1967.

Wassily Kandinsky, *Point to Line to Plane* (tr. Hilla Rebay). Guggenheim Museum, 1947.

Georgy Kepes, ed., *The Language of Vision*. Paul Theobald, 1951.

The Nature and Art of Motion. Braziller, 1965.

Richard Kostelanetz, ed., *On Contemporary Literature*. Avon, 1964.

Siegfried Kracauer, *Theory of Film: The Redemption of Physical Reality*. Oxford University Press, 1960.

Charles Lapicque, *Essais sur l'espace, l'art et la destinée*. Grasset, 1958.

Samuel Levin, *Linguistic Structures in Poetry*. The Hague, Mouton, 1962.

Richard McKann, ed., *Film: A Montage of Theories*. Dutton, 1966.

Marianne W. Martin, *Futurist Art and Theory, 1909-1915*. Oxford, Clarendon Press, 1968.

Henri Meschonnic, *Pour la poétique*. Gallimard, 1970.

Lázló Moholy-Nagy, *Vision in Motion*. Chicago, Paul Theobald, 1947.

Noel Mouloud, *La Peinture et l'espace: recherches sur les conditions formelles de l'expérience esthétique*. PUF, 1964.

René Nelli, *Poésie ouverte, poésie fermée*. Cahiers du Sud, 1947.

Vladimir Nilsen, *The Cinema as a Graphic Art (On a Theory of Representation in the Cinema)*. London, Hill and Wang, 1937.

Stephen Pepper, *Principles of Art Appreciation*. Harcourt, Brace, 1949.

Works Referred to or Consulted

Renato Poggioli, *Poets of Russia, 1890-1930.* Cambridge, Harvard University Press, 1960.

Ezra Pound, *Instigations;* together with Ernest Fenellosa, *An Essay on the Chinese Written Character* (1920), reprinted, Freeport, N.Y., Books for Libraries Press, 1967.

Lee T. Lemon and Marion J. Reis, *Russian Formalist Criticism.* Lincoln, Nebraska University Press, 1965.

Jean-Louis Schefer, *Scénographie d'un tableau.* Seuil, 1969.

Roger Shattuck, *The Banquet Years: The Arts in France 1885-1918,* Harcourt, Brace, 1955.

Philippe Sollers, *Logiques.* Seuil, 1968.

Léon Somville, *Devanciers du surréalisme: Les groupes d'avant-garde et le mouvement poétique 1912-1925.* Geneva, Droz, 1971.

Francis Steegmuller, *Apollinaire: Poet Among the Painters,* Farrar, Straus, 1963.

George Steiner, *Language and Silence: Essays on Language, Literature, and the Inhuman.* Athenaeum, 1967.

Wylie Sypher, *From Rococo to Cubism in Art and Literature.* Random House, 1960.

Joshua Taylor, *Futurism,* Museum of Modern Art, 1962.

E.M.W. Tillyard, *Poetry Direct and Oblique.* London, Chatto and Windus, 1934 (reprinted 1966).

W. K. Wimsatt, *The Verbal Icon: Studies in the Meaning of Poetry.* Lexington, University of Kentucky Press, 1954 (new edition, 1967).

Peter Wollen, *Signs and Meaning in the Cinema.* Bloomington, University of Indiana Press, 1969.

INDEX

The key words for this study, those used with the greatest frequency, are not included in this list since they are found virtually everywhere: Dada, surrealism, canvas, screen, scene, text, theatre.

PRINCETON ESSAYS IN EUROPEAN
AND COMPARATIVE LITERATURE